Henry VIII

These and other titles are included in The Importance Of biography series:

Maya Angelou
Louis Armstrong
Neil Armstrong
James Baldwin
Lucille Ball
The Beatles
Alexander Graham Bell
Napoleon Bonaparte
George W. Bush
Julius Caesar
Rachel Carson
Fidel Castro
Charlie Chaplin
Charlemagne
Winston Churchill
Hillary Rodham Clinton
Christopher Columbus
Leonardo da Vinci
James Dean
Charles Dickens
Walt Disney
Dr. Seuss
F. Scott Fitzgerald
Henry Ford
Anne Frank
Benjamin Franklin
Mohandas Gandhi
John Glenn
Jane Goodall
Martha Graham
Lorraine Hansberry

Ernest Hemingway
Adolf Hitler
Thomas Jefferson
John F. Kennedy
Martin Luther King Jr.
Bruce Lee
Lenin
John Lennon
Abraham Lincoln
Charles Lindbergh
Douglas MacArthur
Paul McCartney
Margaret Mead
Golda Meir
Mother Teresa
Muhammad
John Muir
Richard M. Nixon
Pablo Picasso
Edgar Allan Poe
Queen Elizabeth I
Franklin D. Roosevelt
Jonas Salk
Margaret Sanger
William Shakespeare
Frank Sinatra
Tecumseh
J.R.R. Tolkien
Simon Wiesenthal
The Wright Brothers
Chuck Yeager

THE IMPORTANCE OF

Henry VIII

by Marilyn Tower Oliver

LUCENT
BOOKS ®

THOMSON

GALE

San Diego • Detroit • New York • San Francisco • Cleveland • New Haven, Conn. • Waterville, Maine • London • Munich

LIBRARY OF CONGRESS CATALOGING-IN-PUBLICATION DATA

Oliver, Marilyn Tower.
   Henry VIII / by Marilyn Tower Oliver.
     p. cm. — (The importance of)
   Includes bibliographical references and index.
   Contents: A royal childhood, 1491–1509—The young king brings promise of new prosperity, 1509–1513—Political intrigues and a lust for power, 1514–1523—The death of a cardinal and the king's "great matter," 1520–1530—Henry defies the church, 1530–1535—To arouse the king's anger means death, 1535–1540—The final years, 1540–1547.
   ISBN 1-59018-424-6 (hardback : alk. paper)
  1. Henry VIII, king of England, 1491–1547—Juvenile literature. 2. Great Britain—History—Henry VIII, 1509–1547—Juvenile literature. 3. Great Britain—Kings and rulers—Biography—Juvenile literature. [1. Henry VIII, king of England, 1491–1547. 2. Kings, queens, rulers, etc. 3. Great Britain—History—Henry VIII, 1509–1547.]
I. Title. II. Series.
   DA332.O45 2004
   942.05'2'092—dc22
                                      2003021392

Printed in the United States of America

Contents

Foreword

THE IMPORTANCE OF biography series deals with individuals who have made a unique contribution to history. The editors of the series have deliberately chosen to cast a wide net and include people from all fields of endeavor. Individuals from politics, music, art, literature, philosophy, science, sports, and religion are all represented. In addition, the editors did not restrict the series to individuals whose accomplishments have helped change the course of history. Of necessity, this criterion would have eliminated many whose contribution was great, though limited. Charles Darwin, for example, was responsible for radically altering the scientific view of the natural history of the world. His achievements continue to impact the study of science today. Others, such as Chief Joseph of the Nez Percé, played a pivotal role in the history of their own people. While Joseph's influence does not extend much beyond the Nez Percé, his nonviolent resistance to white expansion and his continuing role in protecting his tribe and his homeland remain an inspiration to all.

These biographies are more than factual chronicles. Each volume attempts to emphasize an individual's contributions both in his or her own time and for posterity. For example, the voyages of Christopher Columbus opened the way to European colonization of the New World. Unquestionably, his encounter with the New World brought monumental changes to both Europe and the Americas in his day. Today, however, the broader impact of Columbus's voyages is being critically scrutinized. *Christopher Columbus*, as well as every biography in The Importance Of series, includes and evaluates the most recent scholarship available on each subject.

Each author includes a wide variety of primary and secondary source quotations to document and substantiate his or her work. All quotes are footnoted to show readers exactly how and where biographers derive their information, as well as provide stepping stones to further research. These quotations enliven the text by giving readers eyewitness views of the life and times of each individual covered in The Importance Of series.

Finally, each volume is enhanced by photographs, bibliographies, chronologies, and comprehensive indexes. For both the casual reader and the student engaged in research, The Importance Of biographies will be a fascinating adventure into the lives of people who have helped shape humanity's past and present, and who will continue to shape its future.

IMPORTANT DATES IN THE LIFE OF HENRY VIII

1502
Prince Arthur dies;
Henry becomes
Prince of Wales.

1491
Henry Tudor, the
second son of Henry
VII and Elizabeth of
York, is born on
June 28.

1509
Henry VII dies;
Henry and
Catherine of
Aragon marry;
coronation of
Henry as king
of England.

1519
Henry Fitzroy,
illegitimate son
of Henry and
Elizabeth
Blount, is born.

1516
Mary, daughter of
Henry and Queen
Catherine, is born.

1495	1500	1505	1510	1515	1520

1501
Catherine of
Aragon and
Henry's brother,
Arthur, Prince of
Wales, marry.

1513
Henry's army
captures the
French towns
of Therouanne
and Tournai.

1520
Field of the
Cloth of Gold
takes place in
France with
Henry and
Francis I;
Henry takes
Mary Boleyn
as his mistress.

1503
Princess Margaret, Henry's
older sister, marries King
James IV of Scotland.

1514
Mary, Henry's younger
sister, marries Louis XII
of France.

1515
Mary marries Henry's best friend,
Charles Brandon, Duke of Suffolk.

1521
Henry writes his book *Assertio* defending the Catholic Church and presents it to the pope, who rewards him with the title of Defender of the Faith; Henry dubs Thomas More a knight.

1533
Henry and Anne Boleyn marry in late January; in March Parliament passes Act in Restraint of Appeals, ruling that all spiritual matters will be decided in England rather than in Rome; Anne Boleyn is crowned queen of England on June 1; Elizabeth, daughter of Henry and Anne Boleyn, is born September 7.

1536
Catherine of Aragon dies; Anne Boleyn is executed; Henry and Jane Seymour marry.

1537
Edward (later King Edward VI), son of Henry and Jane Seymour, is born; Jane Seymour dies.

1540
Henry and Anne of Cleves marry (it is annulled six months later); Henry and Catherine Howard marry.

1525	1530	1535	1540	1545	1550

1529
Cardinal Wolsey is accused of treason.

1530
Cardinal Wolsey dies.

1532
Parliament passes a law called Submission of the Clergy, which requires church laws to be approved by the king; Sir Thomas More resigns as lord chancellor; Queen Catherine is ejected from the court.

1534
The Act of Supremacy recognizes the king as head of the church, creating the Church of England; the Act of Succession validates the marriage of King Henry VIII and Anne Boleyn and declares their children as heirs to the throne.

1541
Margaret, Henry's older sister, dies.

1542
Catherine Howard is executed.

1543
Henry and Catherine Parr marry.

1547
Henry VIII dies on January 28.

A King Without Equals

King Henry VIII was one of the most significant monarchs in English history, a man whose influence extends more than five hundred years. Born during the transition between the Middle Ages and the Reformation, he took a medieval kingdom and built the foundations of a modern state.

Henry VIII's life and the lives of those who were close to him were so filled with drama and controversy that they have been the subjects of many novels, plays, and movies. He is perhaps best known for his six wives. The poem "Divorced, beheaded, died . . . divorced, beheaded, survived,"[1] which circulated during Henry's life and after, describes the fate of his wives. In order to marry his second wife, he separated England from the Roman Catholic religion, creating the Church of England. His reign, however, was characterized by much more than the problems endured in his personal life.

During Henry's lifetime, he was both loved and hated by his subjects and courtiers. As a young man, he was considered the richest, most attractive, and most accomplished monarch in Europe. His talents included writing music and poetry, dancing, superb athleticism, and proficiency in French and Latin. His wide interests included mapmaking, astronomy, and clock making, and his patronage of these disciplines laid foundations for future developments in their technology.

These accomplishments, however, are contrasted with dark moments, which are part of what make his life fascinating. For example, he had a large personal library and was the first English king to write and publish a book, but he was also responsible for the destruction of many libraries and rare books owned by monasteries and convents. Although as king he wrote about the importance of living an honest, virtuous life, he also spent much time on senseless wars and lavish festivities.

Even his many marriages cannot be simply explained by his fickleness or simple lust. Although he had many wives in the second half of his life, during the first part of his reign he was more or less faithful to his first wife, Catherine of Aragon, for over twenty years. A man of passions, his later marriages were motivated not only by the sexual attractions of much younger women but also by the desperate necessity of a male heir to succeed him as king and to carry on the Tudor dynasty. Although Henry seemed to love his two daughters, especially when they were very young, he believed that only a son would secure the throne and provide stability in English leadership. Up to that time, a queen had never ruled England.

Europe in the First Half of the Sixteenth Century

At the beginning of Henry's reign, England was a minor power compared to Spain and France, both of which had larger populations. England's principal enemy was France, and from time to time, English kings asserted their belief that they should also rule the French. England also faced an enemy in Scotland, which was a separate country ruled by its own king. Border wars between England and Scotland would be a major concern during Henry's reign.

King Henry VIII of England was one of the most influential European monarchs of the sixteenth century.

Three monarchs, Francis I of France, Emperor Charles of the Holy Roman Empire, and Henry VIII, vied to become the most dominant ruler in Europe, and their struggles for power created instability and warfare throughout much of the first half of the sixteenth century. The pope in Rome was the supreme authority in matters of religion, but he also was involved in Europe's political affairs. Henry's relationships with these rulers, who were at times his allies and at other times enemies, shaped much of his reign. The result was an ongoing undercurrent of intrigue, jealousy, and hostility.

Religious beliefs and philosophical ideas about the role of leadership also created tensions and violence. At the beginning of the sixteenth century, Roman Catholicism was the dominant religion in Europe, and the church's power was absolute. In 1516, however, a German priest named Martin Luther challenged the authority of the church and laid the groundwork for the Protestant Reformation that would transform parts of northern Europe. The struggles between those who followed the new ideas and those who were unwilling to give up the old resulted in bloodshed and violence. Henry VIII, who was fervently interested in religious ideas, intensely disliked the ideas Luther espoused and severely punished any who followed him. Ironically, despite the fact that he disapproved of Luther's ideas, Henry himself eventually broke from the Catholic Church. By declaring that the king, not the pope in Rome, was the supreme authority in English religion and politics, Henry separated England from Rome, creating the Church of England. Although his motives were more personal and political than spiritual, he did create a new denomination that still exists today.

AN ABSOLUTE RULER

Henry could be charming, but he was also stubborn, unreasonable, and ruled absolutely. He was a man of his times, however; in the sixteenth century, most monarchs and their subjects believed that a king received the right to govern from God. Known as the divine right of kings, this principle created oppressive governments in which any dissension was considered treason, punishable by death. Author E.W. Ives in the book *Anne Boleyn* explains: "In the sixteenth century power was exercised by the ruler in person, or by direct delegation; this was the reality in England and in Europe alike. Policy was what he [the king] decided; advancement and honour was at his gift; his person in fact personifies the community. . . . The ultimate demand on any subject was to be called to obey."[2]

Although Henry did not question his divine right to be king, he also used Parliament, England's legislative body, to pass new laws regarding the church and the order in which his children would follow him as leader. Using Parliament in such a fashion laid the foundation for a more representative form of government still enjoyed by England today.

1 A Royal Childhood, 1491–1509

The birth of a royal baby has always been a welcome event in England, so the arrival of Henry Tudor, who was born on June 28, 1491, was a cause for celebration. He was the second son and third living child of King Henry VII and Elizabeth of York. Because many children born in the fifteenth century did not survive infancy, the birth of a backup heir to the throne was important to the continuity of the royal line. Having sons to inherit the throne was particularly important to the Tudor family because their ascent to the English throne was recent and somewhat insecure. The new baby's father, Henry VII, had become king six years earlier in 1485 after he had defeated his distant relative, King Richard III, at the Battle of Bosworth Field. Richard's death and the Tudor victory ended a long period of civil unrest—called the Wars of the Roses—between two factions of nobles. The name came from the symbols of the two rivals: The Tudors were of the house of Lancaster, and their emblem was a red rose; their rivals from the house of York used a white rose as their symbol. The marriage of Henry's parents, Henry VII and Elizabeth of York, united these two factions. Unrest and intrigue still plagued the country, but the alliance brought a period of relative peace to England after many years of bloody warfare.

Although the new baby would be second in line to the throne of England, following his brother Arthur who was older by five years, his birth was celebrated with an elaborate christening at Greenwich at the Church of the Observant Friars, where he was named Henry, in honor of his father. The christening of a royal child followed a strict protocol. The water had to come from the baptismal font from Canterbury Cathedral (almost one hundred miles from Greenwich), and it was required that the infant be christened in full view of those in attendance. To help out in the royal nursery, extra servants were brought in, and four special attendants, called rockers, were named to rock and comfort the infant.

The baby's appearance resembled that of his mother. The infant Henry had a broad forehead, pink cheeks, and golden hair. He was a healthy, sturdy child unlike his more delicate older brother.

A PRECOCIOUS CHILD

Prince Henry was barely out of infancy when he began receiving honors acknowledging

THE WARS OF THE ROSES

During the years immediately before Henry VIII's birth, England had experienced a violent period known as the Wars of the Roses. The wars were named for the symbols of the two warring sides, the Yorkists and the Lancastrians, who were related by their descent from a common ancestor, Henry VIII's great-grandfather, King Edward III, who ruled England from 1327 to 1377. The emblem of the house of Lancaster was a red rose, and that of the house of York was a white rose. As king, Edward declared his right to also rule France, which he invaded, capturing the port of Calais in 1347. The Lancastrians ruled England from 1399, but when King Henry VI became ill in 1453, the Duke of York was declared protector of the kingdom. When Henry's health improved, he reclaimed the throne, but the Yorkists refused to give up power, setting the stage for the feud between relatives. The Yorkists placed one of their members, Edward IV, on the throne in 1461. In 1483 Edward IV's brother, Richard III, murdered his young nephew, heir to the throne, and seized the throne for himself. Henry VIII's father, Henry VII, who had been living in exile in France, returned to England in 1485 and defeated and killed his cousin Richard at Bosworth Field, ending the wars. He declared himself king and made peace by marrying Henry VIII's mother, Elizabeth of York, establishing the Tudor dynasty.

At the time of Henry VIII's birth in 1491, the Tudor dynasty had held power for only six years, and there were many who challenged its authority both in England and abroad.

The marriage of Henry VIII's father, Henry VII (right), and his mother, Elizabeth of York, ended the Wars of the Roses.

his importance in the royal line of succession to the throne of England. The ceremonies surrounding the granting of the honors were significant because they confirmed the importance of the Tudor reign. Before he was two years old, Henry received a number of impressive ceremonial titles including that of Constable of Dover Castle. In 1494, when he was three years old, Henry received even more important honors during an elaborate three-day ritual. The little boy was placed on a large warhorse and was led to Westminster, where he was greeted by the mayor of London and other important dignitaries. He then underwent a long initiation during which he was made a knight of the Bath, which was a prestigious rank for British nobility. During this ceremony, Henry was given a ceremonial bath. The next day, spurs were put on his heels as his father dubbed him a knight of England. Appearing in front of the king and the nobles of Parliament, the little boy was given the impressive titles of Duke of York, lieutenant general of Ireland, marshal of England, and warden of the Cinque Ports, and he was granted an income of one hundred pounds a year. These titles brought money into the royal treasury and kept the power of those positions within the royal family. Tournaments and celebrations were held in honor of Henry's assumption of these titles.

Henry was an intelligent child. From early childhood he showed a great talent for music, which he enjoyed throughout his life. As a child, he had his own minstrels who played for him. He also learned to play the lute, the organ, and the harp-

As a child, Prince Henry received many honors and titles that kept many positions of power within the Tudor family.

sichord, and he wrote music, which was highly regarded at the time.

The court of Henry VII and Queen Elizabeth was a lively place. Humor was provided by court jesters named Scot, Dick, Patch, and Diego. Traveling dancers and magicians often came to court to entertain the royal family and their nobles. Henry was also exposed to a variety of animals, with the Tudors maintaining large stables with horses and mules. Exotic animals such as lions and leopards were kept at the Tower of London. Hunting was a popular sport, and Henry's father taught his children to shoot with a longbow.

THE CHILDREN OF THE ROYAL FAMILY

Queen Elizabeth gave birth to seven children in all, but three died in infancy or at a young age. By 1497 four children, Arthur, Margaret, Henry, and Mary, had survived. The children were blond, and unlike their pale older brother Arthur, Henry, Margaret, and Mary had ruddy complexions. As Henry grew up, his hair turned to a darker auburn. All four children were dressed in miniature adult clothing.

Henry, who enjoyed hearty good health, was an energetic and active boy. Like Henry, his older sister, Margaret, had a lively temperament. From early childhood she had been destined to marry the king of Scotland. Mary, his younger sister, was a vivacious and beautiful child.

Henry and Mary were very close friends throughout their childhood, but little is known about his relationship with his older brother. By the time Henry was old enough to be friends with Arthur, the prince had been sent to live on the Welsh border, and the two would only see one another on special occasions such as Christmas.

For most of the year, the three younger children lived in the royal nursery at Eltham Palace near London. Henry, who had a mercurial temperament, had his own fool, a jester named Goose, who entertained him when he became moody. Their diet was rich, and all their food was seasoned with sugar or honey. Meals were washed down with alcoholic drinks such as wine or beer because the water was polluted and unsafe to drink.

Although the children lived in royal palaces, they were for much of the year cold, damp places that were warmed by fireplaces. Biographer Carolly Erickson writes:

> Carpets of rushes and sweet herbs caught most of the spills and filth that fell on the floor, but even when these were changed as frequently as the king's regulations required the rooms stank after only a few weeks of use, and the household had to move on to another residence. There was no plumbing, only wooden privies kept covered by a "fair cushion" and a green cloth. At night the wardrober brought in a "night-stool and urinal-at-need." Cleanliness as we understand it was all but impossible. Expensive tallow or olive-oil based soaps were available in wealthy households, but the fleas and bugs that lived in the walls and bred in the folds of clothing infested even the cleanest bodies. Mulberry twigs tied in bunches under the bed helped to keep fleas away at night, but during the day the best that even the king could do was wear a little piece of fur next to his skin to attract all the vermin to one spot.[3]

EARLY SIGNS OF LEADERSHIP

It was expected that the royal children would learn the protocol of the court, and they were often present when important visitors came to see the king. At an early age, Henry was aware of the importance of his position as a royal. When he was seven, he was the guest of the town of London. Because of the fear of illness, officials ran beggars and anyone who appeared to be sick out of the city during the prince's visit. The citizens who remained cheered the young prince, who gave a speech thanking the officials of London for their kindness.

By the time Henry had reached the age of eight, his leadership abilities had been noticed by many. In the summer of 1499, Erasmus of Rotterdam, one of the most famous scholars of the period, visited London and was presented to Henry. Later the scholar remarked on Henry's dignity, courtesy, and royal manner. Erasmus wrote: "When we came into the hall, the attendants . . . were all assembled. In the midst stood Prince Henry, . . . and having already something of royalty in his demeanor, in which there was a certain dignity combined with singular courtesy."[4] Henry began to correspond with Erasmus in Latin.

THE EDUCATION OF A PRINCE

Henry received his education as one of a group of noble children, which included his sisters Margaret and Mary. As the second son, Henry was educated to possibly become a high official of the Catholic Church. He was assigned a tutor, John Skelton, to ground him in the classics and languages. Skelton was a scholar, a poet, and a priest, and he taught his young student Latin. Because Latin was the language of international diplomacy in the early sixteenth century, noble children were expected to learn it at a young age. Another scholar taught Henry French, the language used in many European courts. By the time Henry was eight, he was proficient in both languages, and when he was ten he read Skelton's essay in Latin about the duties and expectations of a prince. Skelton was

DESIDERIUS ERASMUS

Desiderius Erasmus was considered one of the greatest scholars in Europe during the sixteenth century. He was born in Rotterdam, Holland, in 1469, the illegitimate son of a priest and a physician's daughter. In spite of this, he received the best education available to a young man at that time. He entered a monastery and was ordained as a priest in 1492. Erasmus studied at the University of Paris and traveled around Europe, visiting England where he met the young Prince Henry, with whom he was very impressed. While in England he made lifelong friends with other intellectuals such as Sir Thomas More.

Erasmus wrote a number of books including *Adagia,* a collection of Greek and Roman proverbs, *Handbook of a Christian Knight,* and *Praise of Folly.* An independent thinker, he rejected both Martin Luther's ideas of predestination and the powers claimed for the pope. He tried to free scholarship from the church and from the more rigid ideas of the Middle Ages. His opinions and advice were sought by many of the most powerful men of his time, including Henry VIII. Erasmus died in Switzerland in 1536.

also a gifted musician who sang his poems while accompanying himself on the lute. Henry's lifelong fondness for folk songs probably came from singing them with his teacher.

In addition to his formal education, Henry had many other interests. He loved to experiment with mechanics and enjoyed designing weapons and forts. He was also gifted in mathematics and was especially fascinated by astronomy. His specially designed astrolabe, an instrument used to study the stars, is in the British Museum. Geography was also a lifelong interest that started in childhood, and he had a collection of maps and mapmaking materials.

Henry's day would begin early in the morning when he would attend early mass. The morning would include studies in Latin, Greek, and French. He would also study pen-

Henry learned to be an excellent horseman at a young age in order to pursue his interests in jousting (pictured) and hunting.

manship, mathematics, and logic. His study of English history, including the successful French invasion of England by William the Conqueror in 1066 and later instances of English kings waging wars on French lands, fueled Henry's dreams of someday fighting France. In the afternoon he would learn jousting, sword fighting, and hunting. Because these activities required skill as a horseman, he also was trained to be a very good rider who could mount and dismount without using stirrups. These activities were followed by a light meal in the late afternoon. After music and dancing lessons, the evenings were spent playing chess or gambling with other noble children. One of these nobles, Charles Brandon, would be a lifelong friend.

HENRY'S GRANDMOTHER, MARGARET BEAUFORT

Another noble with great influence in Henry's childhood was his paternal grandmother, Lady Margaret Beaufort. It is believed that she was instrumental in selecting John Skelton as his tutor. Lady Margaret exercised absolute authority in the royal nursery, where she supervised the children's diet and education. An educated woman herself, she had a large library of books in French and English. She was both stern and affectionate with her grandson. Of all the royal children, Henry was her favorite, and when he was ten, she had chosen him as heir to her fortune.

It is believed that Henry's intellectual and religious interests came from his grandmother. When he was king, he made sure

that his own court followed the same rules that she formed for running the royal household and its nurseries.

A ROYAL MARRIAGE

In the fifteenth and sixteenth centuries, royal children had little choice as to whom they would marry. Engagements were made to further political alliances with other royal families in Europe, and they often took place when the children were very young.

In 1501, after lengthy negotiations that had begun in 1496, plans were made for the marriage of fifteen-year-old Arthur and sixteen-year-old Catherine of Aragon, the daughter of King Ferdinand and Queen Isabella of Spain. The marriage was advantageous for both Spain and England because it would improve the friendship between the two countries and strengthen the position of both nations in relationship to France, which was a threat to the security of both. Henry VII was also eager to receive the rich dowry that the Spanish monarchs promised to give him for their daughter's marriage.

Catherine's arrival in London in the fall of 1501 was a great occasion. She was escorted by four hundred English knights and nobles dressed in red and black riding on horseback. Although the Spanish authorities had demanded that the princess could not be seen by the king or her bridegroom until the wedding day, King Henry VII insisted on visiting her to make sure that she had no defects. He was pleased with her looks, especially her fair coloring and fine complexion. The princess and the king could not communicate, however, as she did not

Catherine of Aragon married Henry's brother Arthur. She was widowed less than six months later when Arthur died of tuberculosis.

dressed in white velvet, escorted the bride down the aisle. Despite the elaborate ceremony, there did not seem to be much attraction between Arthur and Catherine as neither could speak the other's language. Catherine later would claim that the marriage had never been consummated.

Not long after the marriage of Arthur and Catherine, Henry's older sister, Margaret, was engaged to King James IV of Scotland. Their father hoped that the engagement would ease tensions between England and Scotland. All the Tudors except for Prince Arthur, who had been sent to Wales to establish a court, were present for the engagement celebrations.

PRINCE ARTHUR DIES

The marriage of Catherine and Arthur lasted less than six months due to the death of Prince Arthur. Arthur had never had strong health, and it is likely that he died of tuberculosis. His death made Henry the heir apparent to the throne of England.

Because of the importance of an alliance between England and Spain, King Henry and King Ferdinand and Queen Isabella began negotiations to arrange a marriage between Prince Henry and Catherine. Henry's father was interested because the dowry promised by Spain for the marriage between Catherine and Arthur had not yet been paid to him in full. The engagement, however, would require a special dispensation or permission from the pope because it was against church law for a woman to marry her dead husband's brother. The dispensation was granted by Pope Julius II in 1504.

speak English or French and he did not speak Spanish.

Ten-year-old Prince Henry was given the job of escorting Catherine into the city of London. Following Spanish custom, she rode a mule. The people of London cheered as she passed by.

The wedding was held at St. Paul's Cathedral two days after her arrival, on November 14, 1501. Prince Arthur was dressed in white satin. The bride was also dressed in white, and she wore a lace mantilla, a silk head scarf worn by Spanish women, which partly covered her face. Prince Henry,

In the meantime, nine months after Arthur's death, Henry's mother, Queen Elizabeth, died following the birth of her seventh child, who also did not survive. To cement relations with Spain and secure Catherine's dowry, Henry's father, now a widower, began

King Ferdinand and Queen Isabella of Spain allowed their daughter Catherine and Prince Henry to wed once Henry reached fifteen years of age.

to think that he would marry his daughter-in-law himself. When Queen Isabella strongly objected, he withdrew his plans and finally agreed to an engagement between twelve-year-old Prince Henry and Catherine, who was now eighteen. The marriage would take place when Henry turned fifteen, provided that Catherine's dowry was paid in full by that time.

During the years when Catherine was a widow, Henry VII treated her very shabbily. Often she did not have enough money to feed her household. Henry VII also would not permit her to return to Spain, fearing she would not return and he would have to give back the portion of the dowry that had already been paid. When Catherine's mother, Isabella, died in 1504, Catherine suffered another setback. The marriage of her parents had unified the Spanish kingdoms of Aragon and Castile. Upon her mother's death, the crown of Castile passed to Catherine's sister, making Ferdinand less important as a ruler. King Henry moved to invalidate the engagement between Catherine and his son, while seeking a more advantageous marriage for Prince Henry, possibly with a French princess.

KING HENRY VII AS MENTOR FOR THE YOUNG PRINCE

Prince Henry had a strong mentor in his father, who groomed him to rule. From observing his father, the prince learned statesmanship and the style of ruling a country. By observing the older man's obsessions and fits of irritability, he also learned that a king could use his temper to cower his opponents.

At age forty-seven, the king's health was failing, and the courtiers surrounding him took care to protect young Henry as heir to the throne. The prince was forcibly kept in seclusion as a way to protect him from the sweating illness that became an epidemic in 1508. The illness, which was probably a form of influenza, struck without warning and caused the victim to perspire heavily and run a high fever. Within a short time after the onset of symptoms, the victim usually died. The courtiers also wanted to make sure that the young prince

---

ENGLAND'S HISTORY OF HOSTILITY TOWARD FRANCE

In the sixteenth century, English dislike and suspicion toward the French had a history dating back to the Norman invasion of 1066. William I, king of England from 1066 to 1087, was born in Normandy, today a province of France. William, the Duke of Normandy, felt that he should also be king of England because of a promise made to him by Edward the Confessor, the king of England and his distant cousin. He promised William that he might possibly inherit the English throne. When this promise was not kept, William prepared for an invasion of England, and in 1066 he conquered the English forces at the Battle of Hastings. He was crowned king on Christmas Day 1066 at Westminster Abbey and then returned to Normandy. Although the English aristocracy led a revolt against the French/ Norman rule, they were unable to win and were replaced by a French-speaking aristocracy.

The hostile feelings toward the French continued through the reign of Henry II, who was born at Le Mans, France, in 1133. Although he was king of England from 1154 to 1189, he spent twenty-one of his thirty-four-year reign in France. The English aristocrats deeply resented competing for power against foreign lords.

Kings of French descent ruled England for several centuries, causing dissension and civil war. King Edward III, a descendant of French kings who ruled England between 1327 and 1377, believed he also had a claim to the French crown and led an attack against the French, who were forced to surrender extensive lands. Between 1337 and 1453 the periodic armed conflicts between the two countries and arguments about who would be king of France are known as the Hundred Years' War. The battles reached a turning point when French king Charles VII reclaimed much of French territory under English control. By the time of Henry VIII, only the port of Calais remained under English rule.

King Henry VII (center) was a mentor to Prince Henry, and he carefully groomed his son to rule one day as king.

was not tempted by harmful influences and vices. For amusement he was permitted outside to practice jousting and to exercise with a select group of friends, but he was always closely watched by his bodyguards.

By the end of 1508, Ferdinand had again become a major power in Europe, and he demanded that negotiations for the marriage between his daughter Catherine and Prince Henry be resumed. Arguments about payment of the remaining dowry continued. Finally Ferdinand insisted that Catherine return to Spain.

Before this could be arranged, in March 1509 King Henry became seriously ill. It is believed that he suffered from tuberculosis. As his final act, he pardoned all criminals except for thieves and murderers, and he put his affairs in order. On April 21, 1509, he died in his palace at Richmond, secure in the knowledge that the crown would pass peacefully to his son.

Biographer N. Brysson Morrison describes the funeral of the king:

As the coffin was lowered into the vault, the heralds took their tabards [short capes] from their shoulders, hung them on the railing round the catafalque [an ornamental platform used in funerals] and lamented, "The noble King Henry the Seventh is dead!" Then they put their tabards on again and with one voice shouted the cry loud with joy, "Long live the noble King Henry the Eight." The new reign had begun.[5]

Prince Henry was now King Henry VIII, ruler of England, Ireland, and Wales.

Chapter

2 The Young King Brings Promise of New Prosperity, 1509–1513

The English people were optimistic and enthusiastic at the prospect of having a young king. Throughout the country there was a feeling of excitement and happiness that the change of leadership had occurred without the bloodshed and fighting that had marked previous royal successions. Henry VII was not greatly mourned. Although he had restored a sense of order to England, he had not been a heroic leader. Young Henry was a dashing figure who would turn eighteen, the age of adulthood, in two months. He was a handsome young man and was taller than most of his countrymen. His subjects were also impressed by his intellectual accomplishments and his athletic skills at jousting and hunting.

One of young Henry's first acts was to order the execution of two of his father's principal tax collectors. The two men, Sir Richard Empson and Sir Edmund Dudley, under orders from Henry's father, had squeezed money from the English people to satisfy Henry VII's greed. The executions pleased the masses and were a way to distance himself from his father's financial policies. They also foreshadowed Henry's later actions in which he would use legal means to get rid of people who displeased him or who stood in his way.

HENRY MARRIES HIS SISTER-IN-LAW

Because it was a king's duty to marry well and produce heirs to the throne, Henry was determined to get married advantageously and quickly. Seven weeks after his father's death, he married his sister-in-law, Catherine of Aragon. The wedding took place in private ceremonies at Greenwich Palace on June 11, 1509, because an elaborate wedding would have been inappropriate so soon after the death of Henry's father. News of the wedding circulated after it had taken place, and Henry's subjects learned that the bride had worn white to show that she was still a virgin in spite of her earlier marriage to Prince Arthur.

THE CORONATION

The coronation of a new king was a very important event. It acknowledged his right to rule, with the expectation that he would receive obedience from his subjects. The much anticipated coronation of Henry and Catherine recognized the new king's divine authority to rule England. In sixteenth-century Europe, kings were considered to rule by divine right. "Princes ought to be obeyed by the commandment of God; yea, and to be obeyed without question,"[6] wrote Stephen Gardiner, who was appointed bishop of Winchester in 1531.

The important event took place two weeks after the royal couple's marriage, on Sunday, June 24, 1509. The ceremony at Westminster Abbey was a magnificent affair with much splendor and pageantry. The streets of London had been decorated with tapestries, and wine flowed freely for everyone.

The royal pair made a magnificent impression. Catherine, wearing an embroidered white satin gown and a jeweled crown, was carried in a golden litter, which swung between two white horses. Her long auburn hair hung loosely down her back, which, according to customs in the sixteenth century, was considered to be a symbol of virginity. Although she was a small woman, she had a regal appearance, and her subjects were impressed by her fair complexion, which was considered the standard of beauty at the time. Henry rode on horseback under a canopy. He was dressed in a golden, close-fitting jacket called a doublet, which was embroidered with precious stones, and a crimson velvet robe trimmed

Prince Henry was crowned king of England in June 1509. The coronation at Westminster Abbey included impressive pageantry and fanfare.

THE YOUNG KING

Some of the best descriptions of Henry as a young king come from the writings of foreign ambassadors to his court. In 1515 the ambassador from Venice, Sebastian Giustinian, wrote about the king's appearance on St. George's Day at Richmond where the court was assembled:

We were ushered into a stately hall. At one extremity was His Majesty, standing under a canopy of gold embroidered at Florence, the most costly thing I ever witnessed. He was leaning against his gilt throne on which was a large gold brocade cushion, where lay the long gold sword of state. He wore a cap of crimson velvet in the French fashion; his doublet was in the Swiss fashion, striped alternately with white and crimson satin, and his hose were scarlet, and all slashed from the knee upwards. Very close around his neck he had a fine collar, from which there hung a round cut diamond, the size of the largest walnut I ever saw, and a very large round pearl. His mantle was of purple velvet lined with white satin, with a train more than four yards in length. Over this mantle was a very handsome gold collar with a pendant of St. George entirely of diamonds. On his left shoulder was the Garter, and on his right shoulder was a hood with a border entirely of crimson velvet. Beneath the mantle he had a pouch of cloth of gold which covered a dagger, and his fingers were one mass of jewelled rings.

in ermine fur. Hanging diagonally across his shoulder and chest he wore a baldrick, or jeweled belt, set with rubies.

The couple, preceded by nobles wearing scarlet gowns trimmed in fur, entered Westminster Abbey on a carpet on which was scattered herbs and flowers. Henry swore to uphold the throne and was then anointed with holy oil. After he was crowned with the crown of King Edward the Confessor, the choir burst forth in song. A heavy crown set with sapphires, rubies, and pearls was placed on Catherine's head, crowning her queen. As the couple left the Abbey to the cheering of the crowds outside, the beating of drums and ringing of bells announced that the coronation had

been completed and that England had a new king and queen.

Following the ceremony, the court returned to Westminster Hall for a coronation banquet and a tournament, which lasted until midnight. The celebrating went on for five days until June 29, when the death of Henry's grandmother, Lady Margaret Beaufort, ended the festivities. To mark her death, he ordered church bells to ring for six days in her honor. Henry had just turned eighteen and was ready to begin ruling his kingdom.

ENGLAND IN 1509

The country Henry now ruled had a population of around 3 million people. About seventy-five thousand people lived in London, the largest and most important city. Westminster, a part of the town located outside the city boundaries of London, was the seat of government and the place where Parliament, the law-making body of England, met when it was summoned by the king. As king, though, Henry controlled all the branches of government including Parliament, which was made up of nobles who did more or less what he wanted. Outside England's borders, a small part of Ireland north of Dublin was under English control. To the north, Scotland was a separate, unfriendly country that was ruled by a king, Henry's brother-in-law, who was allied with France, England's traditional enemy. Dealing with Scotland would present a challenge during most of Henry's reign.

LIFE AT THE NEW KING'S COURT

The early days of Henry's monarchy were filled with frivolity and entertainment. At eighteen, Henry was still young, and he wanted to make up for the confinement he had endured during the latter years of his father's life. He left most of the affairs of state to his advisers so he could pursue his other interests.

Shortly after he became king, he wrote a verse that described his pleasures: "Hunt, sing and dance. My heart is set. All goodly sport. To my comfort. Who shall me let?"[7] Life at the new court was filled with sports, dancing, theatrical events, and tournaments. Henry's days were spent hunting, shooting, jousting, and practicing archery. In the evenings, theatrical spectacles entertained

the court, with Henry often starring in the dances. He and his courtiers wore elaborate costumes made of velvet and satin and trimmed with precious jewels. At one festive party in 1510, Henry and his friend, the Earl of Essex, were dressed as Turks wearing turbans and armed with scimitars.

Music played a large part in the festivities, and Henry often took part singing, dancing, and playing the recorder, the flute, or the virginal, a stringed instrument similar to a harpsichord. A versatile musician, he set his poems to music he composed, and he also wrote masses and ballets.

During this early period of his reign, some of his advisers were critical, saying that the young king was more interested in pleasure than in attending to the affairs of state. For Henry these pastimes were not entirely frivolous. Author Derek Wilson writes:

> He was a natural showman who delighted to flaunt himself before the court, foreign visitors (who would, of course, report back to their own sovereigns) and his people at large. But he understood, perhaps instinctively, the importance of what we would today call "image" and his commitment to visual propaganda was, in itself, a policy statement: here was a monarch who was determined to play a major role in European affairs and who, unlike his father, was "up front" about his intentions.[8]

TRAINING FOR WAR

Jousting and tournaments were another of Henry's great pleasures, and he trained

To prepare themselves for the rigors of battle, Henry and his men trained with two-handled swords, participated in jousting tournaments, and staged mock battles.

daily with the knowledge that the training would help him in future battles. Jousts were a major sporting event that included throwing spears for distance and fighting with two-handed swords, and some tournaments ended with mock battles between two groups of knights. Author Carolly Erickson writes: "The jousts played out Henry's childhood dreams of knighthood, dreams built on medieval tales of romance and courtly adventure. But if mock combats honored the enchanted chivalry of the Round Table, their practical utility was always kept in view."[9]

Henry wanted the young men of his court to be able to fight if necessary. Therefore, he formed an armed guard made up of noblemen who were trained in fighting skills such as archery and the handling of spears and swords. Each was equipped with armor and given two horses, a page, and two archers as assistants.

While the athletic feats involved with jousting and the frequent pageants and

Pregnancy and Childbirth for Noble Women in the Sixteenth Century

During the sixteenth century a woman's principal role in life was to bear children to carry on the family name; therefore, it was important that she be from a family that had many children as it was believed that this would contribute to her fertility. Henry's subjects thought it promising that Queen Catherine's mother, Isabella of Spain, had produced five surviving children who lived to adulthood. Catherine became pregnant shortly after her marriage to Henry VIII in June 1509. Prenatal care as we know it today was nonexistent.

In her book *The Wives of Henry VIII*, author Antonia Fraser writes:

> The "quickening" [when the fetus can be felt moving] of the baby at four months or thereabouts was always an important moment; up to then the midwives were never absolutely sure that they were dealing with pregnancy rather than some other condition. It was not that they did not understand the relevance of a woman's monthly cycle and its stopping; just that hopes of conception were always so desperately keen in high-born ladies that a great deal of unwarranted optimism was encouraged. The quickening of the baby made a hope an established fact.

According to the custom for a royal birth, the queen had to follow a special procedure set during the reign of Henry VII for the birth of a possible heir to the throne. Fraser continues: "A fair pallet bed should be set down beside the ornate royal bed for the actual delivery. All the windows save one were to be covered with richly embroidered arras [tapestries]. And 'No man to come into the chamber, save women.'"

spectacles at court took much of Henry's time, he also knew that one of his most important duties was to produce an heir. He was overjoyed when he discovered that Catherine was pregnant.

Catherine Expects a Child

Henry and Catherine's first baby was expected in May 1510, and great care was taken for the queen's health because both infants and their mothers often died during childbirth.

In late January 1510 the queen went into premature labor long before the baby was due. Catherine's labor was very difficult, but finally she delivered a stillborn girl. At first, those present at the birth did not tell Henry of the baby's death, and preparations for the baptism continued. He had been so determined that the child would be a healthy boy that Catherine feared his anger by her failure to produce a son. Finally, a few weeks later, Henry was told that the baby was a girl who was born dead. Although saddened, he was not unduly worried because he believed that healthy babies would follow.

Catherine was soon pregnant again, and on January 1, 1511, she gave birth to a son. Henry was overjoyed. Throughout London bonfires were set to celebrate the birth, and free wine was passed out to the citizens. The baby was christened with the name of Henry and was given the title of Prince of Wales. Henry made a pilgrimage to a holy shrine to thank God for giving him a son. He also ordered that an elaborate tournament be presented to honor the queen. Henry was a star performer at the event. Unfortunately the baby was weak, and at the end of February he died. His parents were sorrowful, but Henry was confident that Catherine would bear more children.

THOUGHTS OF WAR

Later in 1511 Henry's thoughts turned to war with France. Early in his reign he looked to his father-in-law, King Ferdinand, for advice. Ferdinand, a wily monarch, had his own interests in mind when he tried to convince Henry to join him in waging war against their common enemy, France. Three years earlier King Louis XII of France had invaded Venice, a weak Italian state, in order to plunder its wealth. Ferdinand and Henry were eager to help. Pope Julius II, who in October had formed the Holy League to free Italian lands from the French in order to defend the papacy in Rome. Henry, who believed that the league was a holy cause, was easily persuaded by Ferdinand to invade France in order to provide a diversion while Spain tried to drive the French from Venice. Ferdinand also had his eye on controlling a country called Navarre, which was between

Spain and France. England declared war against France in 1512.

Henry enjoyed the prospect of going to war because in many ways it was like a tournament. However, he preferred leaving most of the detailed planning in the hands of his advisers. One of the most important of these advisers was his chaplain, Thomas Wolsey.

THOMAS WOLSEY

When Henry decided to declare war against France, Thomas Wolsey had the task of preparing the army. A brilliant priest, Wolsey

Thomas Wolsey (right), chaplain to Henry VII, became one of Henry VIII's closest advisers.

was the son of a butcher who had been determined to give his son the education of a gentleman. Wolsey attended Oxford University and decided that the way to success was to become a priest. Wolsey saw that the Catholic Church possessed a great deal of influence in England, and priests were among the king's advisers. Wolsey had joined the court in 1505 as chaplain to Henry VII. After Henry VIII became king, Wolsey continued as an adviser, and by 1511 he had become a member of the king's council.

The king's advisers, who numbered between eight and twelve, depending on the occasion, met to conduct the matters of government. Although the king was the head of the state, Henry rarely attended his advisers' meetings during this period in his life, preferring the pomp and glory of being the king without the responsibilities of actually running the government.

THE FIRST ATTACK

In May 1512 Henry traveled to Southampton to bid farewell to his army, which was to set sail for Spain, where his forces were to join those of Ferdinand to invade France. Henry had decided to remain in England during this venture, but throughout the summer he and Catherine waited for news of the battle. Finally, in October, word arrived that there had been no battle. The English soldiers had spent all summer waiting for the Spanish army to join them, but the Spaniards had set out to capture Navarre instead, leaving the English as a buffer against the French forces who wanted to stop the Spanish invasion. During the hot summer months, the English troops had insufficient food and beer. To quench their thirst, they drank the unfamiliar Spanish wine, which gave them dysentery. Sick and discouraged, the troops became mutinous and wanted to return to England.

When Henry heard this news, he was furious, and he wrote to Ferdinand telling him to cut the throat of any man who tried to leave. It was too late, however, as the troops had already left for England.

Part of Henry's anger came because his pride had been wounded, and he was ashamed by the rumors that were spreading throughout Europe about England's failure to fight. The first military venture of Henry's reign had ended in failure, costing the English a large amount of money and humiliation.

Ferdinand and Henry planned a second invasion of France in 1513 in which Spain would attack from the south and England would cross the English Channel to attack from Calais, its last remaining French possession. This time Henry vowed to lead the troops himself.

THE BATTLE OF 1513

Henry looked forward with excitement and anticipation to his army's departure for France. Elaborate preparations had been made for the troops, who departed on June 30, 1513. Twenty-five thousand oxen had been killed and preserved with salt to feed the men. The warships that would cross the English Channel were loaded with two large field guns and twelve heavy guns

Henry VIII as a Poet

Henry VIII loved to write poetry and lyrics for music, much of which survives today, giving insights into his thinking and ideas. Here is an example of his verses.

Pastime with good company

Pastime with good company
I love and shall until I die.
Grudge who likes, but none deny
So God be pleased, thus live will I.
For my pastance [pastime];
Hunt, sing, and dance
My heart is set!
All goodly sport
For my comfort
Who shall me let?

Youth must have some dalliance,
Of good or ill some pastance.

Company I think then best—
All thoughts and fantasies to digest.
For idleness
Is chief mistress
Of vices all.
Then who can say
But mirth and play
Is best of all?

Company with honesty
Is virtue—vices to flee.
Company is good and ill,
But every man has his free will.
The best ensue.
The worse eschew.
My mind shall be
Virtue to sue
Vice to refuse.
Thus shall I use me!

nicknamed the "Twelve Apostles," which had the figures of various saints cast on their barrels. The crews of the ships were outfitted with coats of green and silver-white, the Tudor colors.

Henry would sail aboard his own ship named *Henry Grace a Dieu*, or as it was commonly known, the *Great Harry*. Catherine, who at first had planned to come on the voyage, remained in England as regent, or deputy ruler. She was again pregnant. Before leaving England, Henry had taken the precaution of having his main rival to the throne, his cousin Edmund de la Pole, who was from the rival York clan, executed.

Thomas Wolsey, who had been in charge of the preparations, also sailed on Henry's boat, along with two hundred attendants.

For Henry the invasion of France was a sort of crusade. The crusades of the Middle Ages had set forth to protect holy sites from being harmed by non-Christians. Defending the Christian faith was a dream Henry had inherited from his father, Henry VII, who had wanted to head a crusade to the Holy Land. Fighting the French who had dared to threaten the security of the pope would be a substitute for going to the Holy Land to fight the Turks. The pope even gave Henry the title the Most Christian King, a title that earlier had been given to the French king and that granted the English soldiers the same status as was given to crusaders.

The idea that he could assist in the triumph of good over evil appealed to Henry's sense of chivalry. Author Carolly Erickson explains:

> "We live in evil times, and the world grows worse instead of better," Henry wrote sadly at the outset of his reign. Fighting on the side of good against the forces of evil was where his duty lay, and from time to time he checked the splendid extravagance of his court when he thought self-denial would further the cause of the right. [10]

THE ENGLISH ARRIVE IN FRANCE

Arriving in English-controlled Calais, Henry's troops were met with celebration and cheers. They stayed in the port city for several weeks to plan the strategy for attack, and soon they were joined by Maximilian I, the Holy Roman Emperor who was also committed to helping the pope. His troops, small in number, fought on England's side in exchange for payment. He also asked that the English attack the fortified French towns of Therouanne and Tournai, which were supposed to belong to his grandson and heir, Charles. Ferdinand, claiming he was too old for war, made a truce with France.

In late July 1513 Henry and his men set forth into hostile French territory. On August 1 they arrived at the walls of Therouanne and began a bombardment using their large guns. The attack continued around the clock with the French returning fire. Henry did not personally take part in the attack, but he openly rode around the camp on his horse, which was decorated with gold bells, practiced archery, and entertained Emperor Maximilian in his pavilion tent.

Ten days into the battle a messenger brought Henry a letter from his brother-in-law, King James of Scotland, who was an ally of the French, ordering Henry to leave Therouanne and France. He warned that the border conflicts between England and Scotland would soon develop into all-out war. Henry was defiant in his response, and he told James he should not think of invading England in his absence.

On August 22 the French retreated, and Therouanne fell. For the king's protection, Henry was held back until the main part of the enemy forces had retreated. Moving on to the town of Tournai, the richest city north of Paris, Henry's forces laid siege, and the town was captured in eight days.

Under Henry's command the English forces had behaved honorably in France. They had not plundered or robbed the French, and French women were treated with consideration. News of his bravery spread throughout England. Although the victories in France did not result in gaining much territory or getting rid of Louis XII, they were a personal triumph for Henry, who had dreamed of glory through battle. Exhilarated by the battles, Henry vowed to go to war again soon.

BORDER DISPUTES WITH SCOTLAND

During the campaign in France, Henry's kingdom faced a serious threat on the northern border with Scotland. In August, King James, at the head of a huge army of Scots, crossed the Tweed River to invade England. He had sold his gold and silver chains to buy ammunition and seven huge guns called the "Seven Sisters." Catherine, who had been left in charge of the country in Henry's absence, quickly raised an army to fight the Scottish forces, and although she was pregnant, she left for the north in hopes of being present at

English and French troops do battle near Therouanne in 1513. Encouraged by victory here, Henry vowed to fight for more territory in France.

the battle. On September 9, 1513, the Scottish army and the English forces fought a fierce battle at Flodden Edge. By the end of the three-hour battle, ten thousand Scots had been killed, including the king and many of his nobles. Catherine quickly sent the news of the English victory to Henry along with James's blood-stained tunic.

Henry was saddened by the death of his brother-in-law because he felt he had died bravely like a king and a soldier, a quality he admired. The victory, however, thrilled him because it reduced the Scottish threat to English security. The French victories enhanced England's position as a power in European politics. He was confident that more victories would follow.

3 Political Intrigues and a Lust for Power, 1514–1523

Henry returned from France in triumph. He had left England as a youthful monarch, but now people referred to him as Great Harry. The victories in France had made England a powerful player in European politics and brought him recognition as a leader to be reckoned with. He also had acquired a taste for war, and before leaving France he had promised the pope that he would return with more troops to conquer the entire country.

THE POPULAR YOUNG KING

Back in England in the winter of 1513–1514, Henry's boundless energy caused him to return to the pursuit of pleasure in the court, where he was regarded with affection and admiration. "He is very popular with his own people, and, indeed with all for his qualities,"[11] said the envoy from Milan.

Shortly after Christmas 1513 the king fell ill with smallpox, but by February he had recovered and was eager to return to fight France. During his convalescence he rewarded the nobles who had served with him in France at a ceremony in which he granted them titles. Among those honored was his best friend and tournament partner,

Charles Brandon, who was named Duke of Suffolk. Wolsey, whose work had made the French campaign a success, was named bishop of Lincoln. The following year, Pope Leo X named Wolsey a cardinal, one of the highest positions in the Catholic Church.

Henry's victories in France established him as a powerful force in European politics.

Wolsey's dream was to ultimately be the first English pope.

PRINCESS MARY AND KING LOUIS XII

Up until 1514 Henry had been politically naive in the treacherous waters of European politics. In March he prepared to invade France again, but Ferdinand and Maximilian, the Holy Roman Emperor, instead signed truces with Louis XII of France. Henry was furious, and because his wife was Ferdinand's daughter, he took out his anger on her. Henry's interest in Catherine, and her influence over him, began to wane from this time.

At Wolsey's urging, Henry reevaluated the upcoming arranged marriage of his sister, Mary, to Ferdinand's grandson, the Archduke Charles of Austria, who was the heir to both Ferdinand's and Maximilian's kingdoms. Breaking the engagement was a way to get back at his former allies. Louis XII was in need of a new wife, since his wife had recently died. Wolsey argued that the marriage of an English princess to the French king would bring peace between the two countries and would add to England's prestige in Europe. If a son were to come from the marriage, the child would be in line to become the next king of France. That Henry agreed to this plan was an indication of how much he had come to rely on Wolsey's advice.

Eighteen-year-old Princess Mary was a great beauty who had no desire to marry the sickly French king. At fifty-two years old, King Louis XII was toothless, pockmarked, and unattractive, and she was in love with Henry's friend, Charles Brandon, the Duke of Suffolk. When she protested the marriage, Henry told her that Louis XII would probably not live too long, and that after his death she would be able to marry whomever she might choose. At any rate, Mary had little choice in the matter, and in October 1514 she married Louis, thus becoming the queen of France. The marriage only lasted for eleven weeks before Louis died and was succeeded by his nephew, Francis I.

Wolsey wrote to Mary telling her not to enter into any new marriage contract without Henry's approval, and Charles Brandon was sent to France to escort her back to England. Henry and Wolsey hoped to renegotiate a marriage between Mary and Charles of Spain. Mary refused to consider this, and she urged Brandon to marry her himself. In spite of his earlier promise that as a widow Mary could marry whomever she pleased, Henry was furious when he learned of her secret marriage in France to his childhood friend, as it did not serve his diplomatic needs.

The couple, fearing that Henry and his council might order Brandon's execution, promised the king the silver plate that had been given to her as queen of France and his choice of her royal jewels. In addition to her dowry, she also promised to pay her brother one thousand pounds a year for twenty-four years. The king then allowed the couple to return to England in Henry's favor.

FRANCIS I

Henry was intrigued by his new rival, King Francis I of France. Like Henry, Francis was

FRANCIS I AND CHARLES V

During much of Henry's life, his two most important rivals for power were the French king, Francis I, and the Holy Roman Emperor, Charles. Francis was born into the Valois family of French kings in the town of Cognac in 1494, and in 1515, at the age of twenty-one, he became king. Henry was very curious about the new monarch and questioned those who had seen him about his appearance; Henry was somewhat vain about his appearance and wanted to be sure that he was the more handsome of the two.

Francis was married to Queen Claude, daughter of the former king Louis XII. As a young monarch, Francis was popular with his people because he stopped abuses by nobles and provided his subjects with games and processions. His reign began with a victory over the Swiss and the capture of the Italian city-state of Milan. As a result he negotiated the Concordat of Bologna with Pope Leo X, which gave the pontiff more power over Catholics in France. Strongly anti-Protestant, Francis severely persecuted those whom he believed guilty of heresy.

Henry's other rival was Charles V, the Holy Roman Emperor and king of Spain. Charles V was Henry VIII's nephew by marriage. The son of the Duke of Burgundy and Queen Catherine's sister Joanna, he inherited most of Belgium, Luxembourg, and the Netherlands from his father, and Spain from his grandparents, Ferdinand and Isabella. After the death of his grandfather, Maximilian I, he was elected the emperor of the Holy Roman Empire, a federation of countries that included much of Germany. The position made him the most powerful ruler in Europe in the first half of the sixteenth century. He dreamed of uniting all of Europe into a great empire.

Charles's dear devotion to Catholicism led him to fight both Protestants who separated from the Catholic Church and the Muslim Turks who threatened to invade Europe from the east. Near the end of his life, he gave the Holy Roman Empire to his brother, Ferdinand I, and the rest of his kingdom to his son, Philip II. He died in Spain on September 21, 1558, and is buried in the Escorial, a palace and monastery northwest of Madrid.

a young monarch. Author N. Brysson Morrison writes of Henry's reaction:

> "The King of France, is he as tall as I am?" he wanted to know. "What sort of leg has he?" came the anxious demand. "Spare," came the welcome answer. Then he opened his doublet [a type of jacket worn in the fifteenth century] and placed his hand on his thigh. "Look here," he invited, "I have a good calf to my leg." On learning that Francis wore a beard, not to be outdone, he allowed his own to grow. It grew in reddish, so with his golden beard he outshone the French King. Thus began a mutual rivalry that was to last for over thirty years.[12]

The death of Spain's King Ferdinand in January 1516 brought Henry another rival for power. The new ruler of Spain was Ferdinand's sixteen-year-old grandson, Charles. Charles was also the grandson of Maximilian, the Holy Roman Emperor, and he stood to inherit a large part of Europe after the emperor's death, ultimately making him the most powerful European monarch.

An Heir to the Throne

Henry still yearned for a child to provide him with an heir to the throne. Catherine had endured many pregnancies, miscarriages, and stillbirths, but she had yet to give birth to a healthy baby. Finally, on February 18, 1516, her sixth pregnancy was successful and the queen gave birth to a daughter who was christened Mary after her aunt. Although Henry was disappointed that the baby was not a boy, he was proud of his daughter and bragged that she never cried. In reply to criticisms that she was not a son, he replied, "We are both young; if it is a daughter this time, by the grace of God, sons will follow." [13]

Although the baby proved that Catherine was capable of producing a healthy infant, Henry still yearned for a son to solidify the Tudors' hold on the throne. England, up to that time, had never been ruled by a queen.

Mistresses

In spite of his happiness at the birth of Princess Mary, Henry was beginning to lose interest in his wife. Although Henry was only twenty-five years old at Mary's birth,

Pope Leo X named Thomas Wolsey (center, left) a cardinal in 1514. Wolsey's ultimate ambition was to become the first English pope.

Catherine was thirty-one, and she was beginning to show her age. Her repeated pregnancies had thickened her figure, and her hair was beginning to turn gray. Although Henry still cared for his wife, he began to have mistresses, which was not unusual in court life. One of his first mistresses was a maid of honor to Princess Mary named Jane Popyncort, who was also a mistress to the duc de Longueville, a French nobleman who had been taken hostage by the English. When she left England to go with him to France, Henry gave her a gift of a hundred pounds. Henry then began to notice a beautiful lady-in-waiting named Elizabeth Blount.

AFFAIRS OF STATE

Meanwhile, Cardinal Wolsey continued to rise as a power behind the throne where he took charge of the day-to-day management of the court. Outwardly, Henry still seemed to be primarily interested in pastimes such as hunting, but his great energy also extended to running many of the affairs of his kingdom.

Author Carolly Erickson writes, "Henry liked to hide the fact that he too worked hard, that like the cardinal he too had a taste for detail and exacting precision. . . . The exact nature of the partnership between Henry and his chancellor was elusive, but there can be no question that all major governmental decisions were the king's, and that his inclinations [also] governed the minor ones." [14]

One of the ways Henry harnessed his great energy was by supervising the con-

Henry staged elaborate pageants to impress foreign ambassadors. Here, the king demonstrates his prowess as an archer at one such spectacle.

struction of a new citadel at Tournai. He discovered a way to save money by hiring soldiers who could also work as laborers.

Diplomacy also drew his interest, and many of the foreign ambassadors to Henry's court were surprised to find him very well informed. The concept of diplomacy, the art of negotiation between countries, was relatively new in Henry's reign. Several countries sent representatives known as envoys to Henry's court. England had sent ambassadors to Spain and Rome as early as 1505.

Henry enjoyed entertaining the ambassadors at dinner, and he often tried to amuse them with spectacular pageants. At one event to celebrate May Day 1515, several Italian ambassadors were invited to Greenwich to observe a pageant in which the king and the court reenacted the feats of Robin Hood. They were impressed to view the maneuvers led by the king, who was dressed entirely in green and accompanied by two hundred archers and one hundred noblemen on horseback.

EVIL MAY DAY

Although Henry was caught up in diplomacy and the intrigues of the court, he did not have a good understanding of the life of his subjects. A current of possible rebellion always ran under the seemingly smooth surface of court life. In spring 1517 the hatred of the people of London toward foreign artisans and merchants was at a high point. Many felt that the king and Wolsey were favoring foreigners by loaning money to them, creating a competition with English workers. On the first of May, violence broke out, and English craftsmen and apprentices attacked the parts of the city where French and Flemish workers lived. The rioters closed the gates of the city so that the king's soldiers could not enter.

When Henry, who was in the town of Richmond, heard of the rioting, he prepared to lead his soldiers against the rioters. In the meantime, royal forces fought their way into London, where they restored order and arrested over four hundred rioters.

Henry ordered that the prisoners be brought before him, condemning them to death. After a period of time, however, he changed his mind and pardoned most of them. About forty were condemned to be hanged, drawn, and quartered as an example. The uprising was known as "Evil May Day."

The same year there was another outbreak of the sweating sickness. It spread rapidly and affected thousands. Bells tolled continuously for those who died, and in one town the illness claimed the lives of half the population. The sickness, which struck rich and poor alike, was most serious in London. The epidemic lasted for months, and many of the royal servants died.

Henry, Catherine, and their infant daughter moved from palace to palace to avoid infection. Even his chief adviser, Thomas Wolsey, who had stayed in London to oversee the government, was stricken with the illness, but he was able to survive it. Henry was pleased that Wolsey had been so devoted to running the country in his absence, but many noticed that the cardinal rather than the king seemed to be in charge.

After the uprising and the epidemic, people had begun to murmur that Wolsey had too much influence on Henry, and there were hints that some were disillusioned with their young king. Many worried that he had not produced a son to succeed him as king, although publically voicing this fear was considered treasonous. Catherine had given birth to her last child, a stillborn baby girl in 1516. Now thirty-one years old, many believed that her childbearing years were over.

CARDINAL WOLSEY'S POWERS GROW

By 1516 Cardinal Wolsey's authority extended into almost every area of English life. He even went so far as to spy on Queen Catherine, and he insisted on knowing how the king spent his money. He controlled all branches of the government and presided over the Star Chamber, a court that had wide authority over both civil and criminal matters. The court's proceedings were marked by secrecy and the absence of a jury. The tribunal's name came from its meeting room at Westminster, which had a ceiling decorated with stars. Throughout his reign, Henry made extensive use of the Star Chamber. The Star Chamber met four days a week, and Wolsey's arrival was marked with pomp and ceremony. Although he rode on a humble mule, he wore robes of red satin with sable trim and was preceded by attendants carrying large gold crosses. Wolsey and Henry often used the Star Chamber to take quick action against their critics and political enemies, but they also used it to enforce laws that other courts, influenced by corruption, could not.

Wolsey desired a lifestyle that rivaled that of the king. In 1515 he had begun construction on a magnificent palace on the

ELIZABETH BLOUNT, HENRY'S MISTRESS

In the sixteenth century it was not unusual for a king to keep mistresses. Sometime around 1514 Henry had an affair with one of the ladies-in-waiting in the court. Although she was commonly called Bessie, her real name was Elizabeth Blount, and she was the daughter of a nobleman, Sir John Blount. She was probably around sixteen years old when she became Henry's mistress. She was considered to be an accomplished girl, known for her singing and dancing. Author Alison Weir, in her book Henry VIII: The King and His Court, *writes:*

Elizabeth Blount featured prominently in a Christmas pageant at Greenwich. She, Elizabeth Carew, Lady Margaret Guildford and Lady Fellinger, the wife of the Spanish ambassador, all dressed up as ladies of Savoy in blue velvet gowns, gold caps, and masks, and were rescued from danger by four gallant "Portuguese" knights, played by the King, Suffolk, Nicholas Carew, and the Spanish envoy. The queen was so delighted with their "strange apparel" that, before they all removed their masks, she invited them to dance again before her in her bedchamber. The King partnered Elizabeth Blount, and there was much laughter when the identities of the dancers were revealed. Katherine thanked the King for "her goodly pastime, and kissed him." It is not known whether Henry and Elizabeth were lovers at this time, but if they were, they were certainly being very discreet about it.

Some writers have suggested that they were not discreet enough, and that the Queen was growing suspicious, because on Twelfth Night, 1515, when the same pageant was staged once again by popular demand, Elizabeth Blount did not appear.

Thames River called Hampton Court. He spared no expense in making it the most lavish residence in England, with 280 guest rooms and rich tapestries, which were changed every week. When Henry was shown around the palace, he was irritated by its splendor, which outdid his own palaces, and asked Wolsey why he had built such an extravagant home. Wolsey glibly explained that he planned to offer it as a gift to the king. Although Wolsey continued to make Hampton Court his home,

Cardinal Wolsey spared no expense in building his palace known as Hampton Court. The lavish residence was designed to rival all of Henry's palaces.

Henry Fitzroy

Henry was delighted when his son, Henry Fitzroy, was born in 1519. But he was sad that as an illegitimate child his son could not inherit the throne. As an infant Henry Fitzroy was taken from his mother, Elizabeth Blount, and installed in his own lavish household. Although he was illegitimate, he would be educated in the manner fitting a king's son. When he was six years old, he was named Duke of Richmond and Somerset, an action that seemed to many in the court a move to place him in line

to the throne. Although he was a young child, he was sent north with the title of lord lieutenant, giving him equality with his sister, the Princess of Wales, who had been sent to a castle on the Welsh border. The young duke lived at Sheriff Hutton in Yorkshire, a few miles north of York. The members of his household wore uniforms of blue and yellow. The title gave him precedent over everyone in the court except his half sister Mary. At one time Henry had considered a marriage between the two half siblings, a suggestion that shocked many people.

Like Henry's other children, Henry Fitzroy was well educated, and in his love of learning, he seemed to take after his father. He was described as sophisticated and handsome.

Born in 1519, Henry Fitzroy was Henry's illegitimate son by Elizabeth Blount.

Henry was not happy until he possessed the deed to the property.

Wolsey also maneuvered the pope into naming him legate. This high rank in the church made him the pope's permanent representative in England and granted him the power to make certain religious decisions to reform the church. One of his acts was to dissolve many of the monasteries and confiscate their wealth for the king.

While Wolsey was managing the government, Henry spent much of his time dealing with his personal affairs. He now had another mistress, Elizabeth Blount, who gave birth to a healthy son in 1519, and Henry eventually acknowledged that the baby was his. The child was named Henry Fitzroy, which means "son of the king," and Wolsey served as his godfather. As was the custom in such affairs, a marriage was arranged for Elizabeth, and the baby was raised out of sight of the court. For Henry, whose court was known in Europe as a model of morality, it was important to maintain appearances, so the birth was at first kept secret.

In 1518 Wolsey drew up an agreement called the Treaty of London, which was signed in October by England and France, binding the two countries to peace for a period of thirty months. The treaty was also signed by twenty minor European countries. In separate treaties, England agreed to return Tournai to France, and Henry's infant daughter, Mary, was engaged to the son of the king of France. It was also agreed that Henry and Francis would meet in France.

The meeting was planned for the summer of 1519, but it was delayed by the January death of Maximilian, the Holy Roman Emperor, which created a shift of power in Europe. Although Maximilian's grandson, King Charles of Spain, would inherit his land holdings, thus becoming the most wealthy ruler in Europe, the prestigious title of emperor was not hereditary. A new emperor would have to be elected.

THE CONTEST FOR THE TITLE OF EMPEROR

Although the title of Holy Roman Emperor was primarily ceremonial, the winner would also rule over a number of German principalities whose nobles elected the emperor. In 1519 King Charles of Spain, King Francis of France, and King Henry all vied for the title of emperor. Pope Leo X, fearing a victory by Charles would make him too powerful, openly supported Francis but secretly encouraged Henry. Both Charles and Francis bribed the electors, but Henry did not. In June the electors chose nineteen-year-old Charles as the next Holy Roman Emperor. The addition of this title to those he already held made him the most powerful monarch in Europe, and he would reign over a kingdom of 16 million subjects in lands that included the Netherlands, Spain, part of Italy, the principalities of Germany, and Austria.

Despite Charles being named Holy Roman Emperor, political maneuvering among the three young kings continued. Henry ruled over less land and fewer people than Charles and Francis, but he would be a significant ally for either of the other rulers. Over the next years, both Francis and Charles would court Henry. Wolsey pushed for a meeting between Francis and Henry, but Queen Catherine urged her nephew, King Charles, to meet with her husband before he could go to France. Wolsey preferred the alliance with France because he was concerned that Spain was already too powerful.

THE FIELD OF THE CLOTH OF GOLD

The meeting between Henry and King Francis, which had been postponed until after the imperial elections, was rescheduled for the summer of 1520. Preparations for the meeting of the two kings were elab-

Henry arrives in Calais, France, to discuss an alliance with King Francis. Because of the lavish preparations for the meeting, it became known as the Field of the Cloth of Gold.

orate, as five thousand people planned to accompany Henry on the trip. The meeting was to take place six miles from the town of Calais in the Val d'Or, or Golden Vale. Henry and his court would stay in a castle in the English-controlled town of Guisnes, and the French would stay in the French town of Ardres. Because the castle at Guisnes was small, six thousand laborers and craftsmen were sent to build an annex. The construction time for the elaborate palace was less than three months. Cost was not spared in the construction of the magnificent building. Elaborate tapestries and hangings of gold and silver decorated the quarters designated for the king and queen, Wolsey, and Mary Tudor, who, although she had remarried, was still considered the widow queen of France. The dining hall had a ceiling of green silk, and taffeta covered the floor. Throughout the

castle the walls were decorated with paintings of the Tudor rose. Because the castle could not accommodate all the nobles, many stayed in the twenty-eight hundred colorful tents nearby.

Huge quantities of food were purchased to feed those in attendance. Reportedly, this included 2,200 sheep; 1,300 chickens; 800 calves; 26 heron; 13 swans; 17 bucks; 9,000 plaice (fish); 700 eels; and an enormous quantity of sugar and cream for pastries.

Behind the scenes Catherine urged Charles to meet with Henry before returning to Spain after his coronation as emperor. The meeting took place at Dover just before Henry was to embark for France. The two had private meetings and discussions for three days, and Henry was pleased because the event marked the first time that a Holy Roman Emperor had visited England.

Twenty-seven English ships left Dover to cross the English Channel for France on May 31, 1520. The summit meeting between Henry and Charles, which came to be known as the Field of the Cloth of Gold, was called by many the "eighth wonder of the world." The meeting began on June 7. Both kings, seeking to impress, were magnificently attired. Henry, wearing heavily jeweled gold and silver clothing and a feathered black bonnet, was mounted on a horse that was decorated with gold bells that jingled as it moved. Francis, also wearing a gold and silver outfit covered with jewels, was accompanied by his Swiss guards. Two weeks of meetings and festivities followed, including tournaments in which three hundred men using blunted swords and lances took part. Although both sides behaved with courtesy, there was an element of hostility beneath the surface. One of the Italian observers wrote, "These sovereigns are not at peace. They hate each other cordially."[15]

It is believed that during the festivities Henry noticed the eldest of two daughters of Sir Thomas Boleyn. The elder, Mary, who earlier in the year had married one of Henry's favorite nobles, William Carey, soon became Henry's mistress. Henry conducted the affair with great discretion.

In spite of the pomp, nothing of substance was accomplished at the meetings of the Field of the Cloth of Gold. A short time later Henry and Charles signed a treaty in which they agreed not to make any new alliances with France for the next two years. In many ways Charles had an advantage over Francis as an ally for England. He was the nephew of Queen Catherine, who was very popular with the English people, and he also was emperor of the Netherlands, an important purchaser of English wool. The English regarded the French with suspicion because of the long history of conflict between the two countries dating from the Norman invasion of William the Conqueror in 1066.

By the end of 1520, Henry had ruled England for close to eleven years. During this time England's status as a political power in Europe had increased, thanks in large part to the maneuvering of Cardinal Wolsey. The mood of his subjects varied between enthusiasm for their young king, who was considered the most handsome monarch in Europe, to irritation at the growing power of Wolsey and the ever-present taxation to finance invasions and war. Also, there was concern that Henry's eleven years of marriage to Catherine had not yet produced the much desired male heir, threatening the stability of the throne.

Chapter

4 The Death of a Cardinal and the King's "Great Matter," 1520–1530

The early years of Henry's reign had been relatively calm, but trouble loomed on the horizon. Some of his subjects were beginning to show dissatisfaction with his rule, and intrigues and challenges to the Crown were afoot.

Returning to England from the Field of the Cloth of Gold, Henry faced a danger to his absolute power as king. A distant relative, Edward Stafford, the Duke of Buckingham, seemed to be maneuvering to place himself as a serious contender to the throne. Because Henry did not have a legitimate son to follow him as king, the duke, who like Henry was a descendant of King Edward III, was a real threat. He was enormously wealthy and had served Henry for many years, but he openly hated and distrusted Cardinal Wolsey. By 1520 Buckingham had gathered a force of men around him, and rumors circulated that he intended to overthrow the king or perhaps assassinate him by stabbing him with a concealed knife.

In April 1521 Wolsey arrested the duke, who was taken to the Tower of London and charged with plotting the death of the king. Four days later he was beheaded, and his vast wealth was given to the Crown. Henry took some for himself and distributed the rest to the nobles who were loyal to him.

The immediate threat to the Tudor power had passed, but Henry knew that without a male heir his position was not fully secure.

DEFENDER OF THE CATHOLIC FAITH

During the winter of 1521, Henry fell sick with malaria. When he recovered, he decided to go on a pilgrimage to thank God for his recovery. Henry was a strongly religious man who was very concerned about the threats to the Catholic Church, which had begun in 1517 when Martin Luther, a German priest, had attacked the church for various abuses. Luther had attracted many followers, especially in western Europe, and his ideas had spread to England. The beliefs, which were called heresies, were against the law, and those that advocated them were burned at the stake.

Henry was very concerned about the heresies because he felt they undermined social stability. His anger led him to write to Pope Leo X, saying that he thought it was his duty to write a book to defend the church. Henry's hidden motive was his desire for the pope to grant him a title such as those that had been given to his rivals.

Henry wrote his book Assertio *to defend the Catholic Church from the heresies of Martin Luther (center). The king hoped his book would carry favor with the pope.*

The pope had named Charles "the most Catholic king," and Francis I was now called "the most Christian king," a title which the previous pope had once bestowed on Henry.

Henry took two years to write his book, titled *Assertio*, which was published in July 1521. A copy, bound in gold cloth, was sent to the pope, who announced his surprise that Henry had time to write a book given the duties of his position. As a reward, Henry received the title of "Fidei Defensor," or "Defender of the Faith." Thomas More, one of Henry's advisers who had helped him write the book, was made a knight and was given the position of under treasurer of the exchequer. More would continue to rise in Henry's government.

DREAMS OF EXPANDING POWER

Three months after the publication of Henry's book, Pope Leo X died. Wolsey, who wanted to be named the first English pope, hoped King Charles of Spain would sponsor him, but his hopes were in vain. Although Charles had twice promised to support Wolsey's candidacy, he betrayed him, and at the last minute backed his former tutor, who became Pope Adrian VI. In spite of his dreams, Wolsey was an unlikely candidate for pope because no Englishman had ever held that position. Nevertheless, he felt betrayed, and his policies became even more pro-France. Henry's sympathies, however, lay with Charles, his nephew-in-law, who had promised to join him in an invasion of France. If the war had a successful outcome, Henry would be made king of France.

To celebrate the alliance, in 1522, Henry agreed to the betrothal of his six-year-old daughter, Mary, to the twenty-two-year-old Charles. It was agreed that the two would marry when she turned twelve. Charles wanted the young princess to be sent to Spain immediately for her educa-tion, but Henry refused, saying she was too young to survive the journey. The two monarchs agreed that in the absence of a male heir, at Henry's death, the eldest son of Mary and Charles would rule England.

PARLIAMENT MEETS

Both Charles and Francis wanted England's support in their struggles for power on the European continent, but since Henry's sympathies were with Charles, Henry declared war against France in 1523, ordering Wolsey to raise funds to pay for an invasion.

Wolsey's first move was to call a meeting of Parliament to ask for money. It was the first time in eight years that the governing body had been called to meet. After

THE ORDER OF THE GARTER

One of the highest honors in England is to become a member of the Order of the Garter, a chivalrous society established by Edward III on St. George's Day, April 23, 1348. The order got its name from an incident when the king gallantly picked up the garter of his dancing partner, the Duchess of Salisbury, which had fallen to the floor. When the bystanders laughed, the king said "Shame on he who thinks evil of it (*Honi soit qui mal y pense*)," which became the order's motto. Membership includes the monarch, the Prince of Wales, and twenty-five knights and nobles. The members meet on St. George's Day to discuss business, elect new members to replace those who died, and to hold a feast. Henry VIII took a great interest in the order during his reign and frequently held meetings at whatever palace he might be staying.

Henry commissioned an illuminated register for the Order of the Garter called the Black Book, which was begun in 1534. It is written in Latin and contains the society's rules, its history, and a record of its ceremonies and elections. The name comes from its black velvet binding.

much argument, Parliament agreed to appropriate less than two-thirds of the amount requested. The monies were raised, but there was bitter complaining throughout the land. The English were not supportive of the war Henry was so eager to wage.

In August a large army left England for France. The troops, under the leadership of Charles Brandon, the Duke of Suffolk,

Henry presides over a meeting of the Order of the Garter. Becoming a member of this chivalrous society is one of the highest honors in England.

planned to attack from the north. By November the English were within fifty miles of Paris, but they turned back because of bad weather, and returned home. Henry was again humiliated in war, but he swore he would try another invasion in 1524.

While Henry dreamed of invading France again, Francis had his eyes on conquering Milan, a territory controlled by Charles. When Francis was captured in Italy, Henry rejoiced. With Francis out of the way, his dream of becoming king of France now seemed a definite possibility. He ordered Wolsey to again raise funds for a new invasion.

THE AMICABLE GRANT

Wolsey's solution was to raise money through a tax called the Amicable Grant, which required Englishmen to pay one-sixth of their wealth to the Crown. The proposal met with great opposition and in some cases, rebellion. When Henry saw how angry the people were, he denied knowledge of the tax, and the Amicable Grant was dropped.

Because criticism of the king was considered treasonous, the people's anger was directed toward Wolsey. Henry continued trying to raise money for the invasion, and he even went to Charles of Spain for the return of funds that Henry had loaned him. Unfortunately, Charles also needed money, and he demanded that nine-year-old Princess Mary be immediately sent to Spain along with her large dowry. When Henry refused, the emperor withdrew his support of the invasion of France and asked to be released from his engagement to Princess Mary so he could marry nineteen-year-old Isabella of Portugal, a princess who had a dowry of millions.

THE NEED FOR A SON AND HEIR

In 1525 Henry was no closer to ruling France. His daughter would not be an empress, and

Princess Mary was Henry's first-born child and the heir to the throne. English tradition, however, required that the monarch be male.

his heirs would not rule over the Holy Roman Empire. More important, he still did not have a son to succeed him as king. The lack of a male heir had become a constant worry for Henry. It was also a concern of his subjects, many of whom believed that God was passing judgment on the king because he had married his brother's wife, an action that was banned in the Bible in the book of Leviticus, which reads, "If a man shall take his brother's wife, it is an impurity; he hath uncovered his brother's nakedness, they shall be childless."[16]

The issue of succession also had political ramifications. Author Carolly Erickson writes:

> From a diplomatic standpoint Henry and England were at a particular disadvantage. With a son he would have been able to arrange a match with the daughter of almost any European ruler he chose, demanding a large dowry and a military alliance in addition. With a daughter he might still gain a military alliance along with a betrothal, but a large dowry would have to be paid out, from his own coffers. And in addition there was the serious question of whether the princess' husband would in time become king of England.[17]

Although it appears that Henry loved his daughter Mary, his official heir, he did not think of her as a serious contender for the throne. Because tradition required that England be ruled by a male, as early as 1522 he began to consider annulling his marriage to Catherine, who was by then past the age of childbearing, to marry a woman who might provide him with a son.

ANNE BOLEYN

Henry began to notice a lively, young lady-in-waiting to the queen named Anne Boleyn, who was the sister of his former mistress, Mary Boleyn.

The Boleyn family was not royal, but it was noble. They were also wealthy. Their ancestors had made a fortune as merchants, who had used their riches to rise in the court. Anne's mother was the daughter of Thomas Howard, the Earl of Surrey, and her father, Thomas, was the oldest son of Sir William Boleyn. When Anne was about twelve, she had been sent to France to be educated, and she had later been a part of the court of Henry's sister, Mary, when she became queen of France. She served in the household of Queen Claude, wife of Francis I.

Anne, or Nan, as she was sometimes called, was not particularly beautiful, and reportedly she had a strawberry mark on her neck, which she hid with a collar band, and a deformity on her left hand that appeared to be the beginning of a sixth finger. Her olive complexion and dark hair did not meet the sixteenth-century English standards of beauty, which favored women who were blond and blue eyed. Her vivacious and charming personality contrasted with that of the serious, religious queen. Anne, who was skilled in dancing and singing, was described in a sonnet written by Sir Thomas Wyatt, one of her admirers, as "Wild for to hold, though I seem tame." [18] Earlier, Anne had been courted by Henry Lord Percy, an heir to great wealth, but the love affair had been discouraged by his father, who felt that he would be marrying beneath him, and by Cardinal Wolsey, in whose household he had been educated. Af-

ter the relationship had been broken up, Anne had gone to the Netherlands. It was after her return in 1525 that she came to Henry's attention.

HENRY FALLS IN LOVE

By 1526 Henry was infatuated with the young woman and described his feelings as his great folly. He was thirty-five years old, which was considered middle age at that time, but he was still handsome and full of energy. Anne, however, refused to enter into an affair as a mistress. She had observed that becoming the king's mistress had not given her sister Mary any additional status. Anne was probably also being advised by her uncle, the Duke of Norfolk, not to become the king's mistress but rather to hold out for marriage and the title of queen.

Henry's infatuation with Anne Boleyn continued to grow. When they were apart, Henry wrote Anne tender love letters, of which seventeen remain in the Vatican Library in Rome; Anne's replies have been lost. In one letter he wrote, "Consider well, my mistress, how greatly my absence from you grieves me; I hope it is not your will that it should be so, but if I heard for certain that you yourself desired it, I could do no other than complain of my ill fortune, and by degrees abate my great folly." [19]

HENRY FITZROY IS GIVEN NEW STATUS

In 1525 Henry had two accidents that brought the need for a successor into sharper focus. While jousting with Charles Brandon, a shattered spear flew into his face. A short time later, he had a serious hunting accident when he tried to jump over a ditch filled with water. Falling from his horse, he landed in the ditch and came close to drowning.

Soon after the incidents, Henry Fitzroy, the king's six-year-old illegitimate son, was brought to court and with much pomp was named Earl of Nottingham and Duke of Richmond and Somerset. These significant titles, which Henry had held as a child, led some to believe that the king might change the law so that Fitzroy could be a successor to the throne despite his illegitimacy. The young duke was given a household with two hundred officers, many servants, and eighty manor houses.

Queen Catherine was very upset at Fitzroy's honors because she did not see a good reason why her daughter, the nine-year-old princess Mary, could not become queen. Her own mother, Isabella, had been queen of Spain, and Catherine had successfully served as regent over England while Henry was invading France. To calm Catherine, Mary was given a household as grand as that of her half brother. Unfortunately, Mary's new home was at Ludlow Castle in Wales, away from the influence of her mother.

Behind the scenes Henry was now plotting for his daughter to marry King Francis,

THE KING'S "GREAT MATTER"

The love affair of Henry VIII and Anne Boleyn was described by many people at the time as the king's "great matter." When they were apart, he wrote her many passionate love letters. Here is one of them as reprinted on English history.net:

My mistress and friend. I and my heart put ourselves in your hands, begging you to have them suitors, for your good favour and that your affection for them should not grow less through absence. For it would be a great pity to increase their sorrow since absence does it sufficiently, and more than ever I could have thought possible reminding us of a point in astronomy, which is, that the longer the days are the farther off is the sun, and yet the more fierce. So it is with our love, for by absence we are parted, yet nevertheless it keeps it fervour, at least on my side, and I hope on yours also, assuring you that on my side the ennui of absence is already too much for me, and when I think of the increase of what I must needs suffer it would be well nigh unbearable for me were it not for the firm hope I have and as I cannot be with you in person, I am sending you the nearest possible thing to that, namely, my picture set in a bracelet with the whole device which you already know. Wishing myself in their place when it shall please you. This by the hand of

Your loyal servant and friend
H. Rex [*Rex* means "king" in Latin]

a move which would make her the future queen of France; however, a delegation from France questioned Henry about the validity of his marriage and the legitimacy of his daughter.

CATHERINE'S FALL FROM POWER

Henry pondered the reasons why all but one of Catherine's babies had been still-born or had died in infancy, and he wondered if the problem was based in their marriage, which went against biblical law. Several prominent churchmen told him that the eighteen-year marriage was not valid and should be dissolved. Henry was torn. One of the principle obligations of a king was to provide a male heir to the throne to guarantee the stability of the country, but it was obvious that he could not fulfill this duty with a wife who was past her childbearing years.

During the 1520s Catherine no longer held the power she had once enjoyed, including not being asked to advise Henry about the affairs of state. Henry was growing tired of her, and he distrusted her connections to Spain and her nephew, King Charles. He decided he could not continue in a marriage that was possibly illegal according to church law, and he seriously began to think of asking the pope to cancel his marriage to Catherine so he could marry Anne Boleyn. He convinced himself that this was a matter of conscience, even though it would make his daughter Mary illegitimate in the eyes of the world.

Biographer Antonia Fraser writes: "He was convinced that the union would *not*

turn out to be free from sin. God had spoken to him through his conscience and would not let him down now. . . . Henry VIII was not the first (or the last) man to equate the law of God with his own deepest wishes."[20]

Henry was confident that the pope would permit ending the marriage. Granting annulments was not an unusual practice for the church, especially for noble people. In fact, several members of Henry's intimate circle, including his brother-in-law Charles Brandon, had received annulments, and his sister Margaret, the widowed queen of Scotland, had divorced a husband so she could marry her lover.

HENRY APPEALS TO POPE CLEMENT

In May 1527 Cardinal Wolsey, as legate, or representative of the pope, set up an official investigation into the matter of the royal wedding, but he kept the proceedings secret from the queen. Wolsey concluded that the annulment would not be as easy to obtain as the king thought because of details in the actual scripture and the wording of the dispensation, which had allowed the marriage in the first place.

In June Henry visited Catherine in her chambers to tell her that he planned to cancel their marriage because they were living in sin. He tried to persuade her to accept this decision and agree to leave the court. Breaking into tears, she adamantly refused to consider a separation because she strongly believed their marriage was fully legal, and she insisted that her mar-

Catherine of Aragon fell out of favor with Henry after failing to provide him with a male heir.

riage to Henry's brother, Prince Arthur, had never been consummated. In July she wrote to her nephew Charles for help in blocking the annulment. Charles was the most powerful ruler in Europe, and he also had control over Pope Clement VII, who at that time was his hostage in Italy. He replied that he would do all he could to help his aunt.

Throughout the summer of 1527, rumors spread throughout London that the king was going to leave his wife to marry a French princess, a liaison that Wolsey had promoted. Behind the scene, Henry busied himself writing tender letters to Anne Boleyn.

When Wolsey left for France on a diplomatic mission, Henry sent a messenger to Rome to ask the pope for permission to marry a second time. The dispensation was granted in December, but it required that Henry be free of his first wife before he could marry again.

Although Thomas Wolsey (right) disapproved of Henry's wish to marry Anne Boleyn (left), he helped Henry obtain an annulment of the king's marriage to Catherine.

When Wolsey returned from France, he was shocked to discover that his king was planning to marry his wife's lady-in-waiting rather than a French princess, as Wolsey had hoped. The affair had become known in England as the king's "great matter." Still, Wolsey was diligent in trying to obtain an annulment of Henry's marriage.

POPE CLEMENT DELAYS HIS DECISION

Henry had placed his fate in the hands of Pope Clement VII, who had followed Adrian VI as head of the Catholic Church. Unfortunately Clement was known for being indecisive when under pressure. In making a decision on the annulment, Clement was being pressured from two opposing forces, the English king, who had the title of Defender of the Faith, and the powerful emperor Charles, who until recently had held him captive in Rome. His response was to delay making a decision to avoid antagonizing either side.

In February 1528 Henry and Wolsey decided to send two representatives to Rome to plead the king's case. The envoys were two young attorneys, Edward Foxe and

Stephen Gardiner. They had orders to convince the pope to support a court that would be held in England under the joint leadership of Cardinal Wolsey and Cardinal Campeggio, an Italian priest who was an expert in church law. Foxe and Gardiner were to use persuasion and, if necessary, threats to get the pope to give Henry what he wanted.

When the two negotiators arrived in Italy, they found the pope living in poverty after his imprisonment by Charles. The pope complained that Henry only wanted the annulment so he could marry Anne. The negotiators answered that Anne was a sober and noble woman and that Catherine would be treated with honor after the annulment. When Clement hesitated, they told him that if Henry did not receive the annulment he desired, he might be forced to leave the church. Finally, the pope agreed to send Cardinal Campeggio to London to try the king's case and make a judgment.

AN EPIDEMIC STRIKES ENGLAND

In spring 1528 there was an outbreak of the sweating sickness, which caused many deaths, especially in London. The country was going through a period of severe economic hardship, and many suffered from a lack of food. To make matters worse, in January, England and France had

---

THE SWEATING SICKNESS

Throughout Henry's reign there were several outbreaks of an illness called the sweating sickness. The malady came on suddenly with headaches and intestinal pains, chills and dizziness. This was followed by a stinking sweat and high fever. Death came to many within hours.

Doctors of the sixteenth century could do little to help. One popular treatment was to bleed the patient. Another was to prescribe exotic medicines, some of which contained gold. It was considered important to keep the patient awake because sleeping while infected was believed to be dangerous. To ward off the illness, people burned spices, and all who could escape to the countryside did so. Drinking vinegar was also believed to prevent the illness and, therefore, was consumed in great quantity by mixing it in sauces and in drinking water. People also carried cloths soaked in vinegar, wormwood, and rose water, which they held before their noses when they came near infected persons.

Henry, who was brave in war and tournaments, feared the sweating sickness, and when the disease broke out, he took refuge in the countryside. He also feared for the health of Princess Mary and his son, Henry Fitzroy, whom he ordered to a remote place away from the epidemic.

---

declared war against the Holy Roman Empire, causing a downturn in the demand for English wool in Flanders, which was part of the empire and an important trading partner. Many blamed Wolsey for the resulting unrest.

To escape the sweating sickness that was striking down many in the court, Henry traveled from household to household. He began to worry about his mortality and spent much time alone. During this time he wrote his will, went to mass daily, and started to write a book called *A Glasse of the Truthe,* arguing that his marriage to Catherine was invalid. Sometimes he would work on the book for hours at a time. His writings convinced him even more that his position about the annulment was a valid one. He looked forward to the arrival of Cardinal Campeggio, a church official that he admired, whom the pope had agreed to send to London in the summer to head a meeting called a decretal commission, which would make a judgment on the legality of Henry's marriage according to church law. Henry and Anne were confident that the judgment would be in their favor.

Unofficially, however, the cardinal had been advised to delay making a decision. At first he tried to persuade the very religious Catherine to enter a convent. When approached about the subject, Catherine listened but said little. A few days later she asked the cardinal to hear her confession in which she insisted that her marriage to Prince Arthur had never been consummated. She stated that she intended to fight the annulment to insure her place as queen and her daughter's claims to the throne.

THE ENGLISH PEOPLE SUPPORT THEIR QUEEN

When Henry tried to gather support from his subjects, he found out how popular Catherine was with the people. Her support from the women was particularly strong, and many gathered outside the palace and cheered for her when she appeared. People were not easily fooled by Henry's arguments in favor of the annulment because they saw him as a man led astray by his love for Anne Boleyn.

In November 1528 Henry gave a public speech about the proposed annulment, saying he would fail in his duty as king if he could not give the country a male heir. He praised Catherine but said he regretted their long marriage because it had caused God's displeasure. The speech, though effective, did not please the queen's supporters.

As 1528 came to a close, both Henry and Wolsey were frustrated and desperate. The decretal commission had failed to reach a decision, and Wolsey knew that a resolution of the problem in Henry's favor was a key to his staying in power. To pressure Pope Clement III to reach a decision, Wolsey sent ambassadors to Rome, but the pope was unsympathetic to Henry's cause. Henry, annoyed at the delay, ordered the commission to proceed with a trial to judge the validity of the royal marriage.

THE QUEEN MAKES AN ELOQUENT PLEA

On June 21, 1529, both Henry and Catherine appeared before the commission and a large

Catherine of Aragon stands before Henry and a commission in 1529. Catherine swore that she had been a faithful and obedient wife.

audience of spectators at Blackfriar's Chamber in Parliament. Henry spoke first, saying he wanted a speedy decision on the validity of his marriage, which he now believed to be sinful. Then Catherine took the floor and addressed the king, saying: "Sir, I beseech you for all the loves that hath been between us and for the love of God, let me have justice and right," she said. "I have been to you a true, honorable and obedient wife . . . ever conformable to your will and pleasure."[21]

Catherine went on to insist that at the time of their marriage she had been a virgin. Saying that she was committing herself to God, she left the court, and when she was called back, she refused to return. In her absence a number of nobles gave testimony, mainly unfounded gossip, about her marriage to Prince Arthur.

The court continued deliberations into July when Campeggio called a recess, and in September he left London to return to Rome. The great matter had not been decided.

WOLSEY'S DOWNFALL

The failure of the commission to reach a decision reflected badly on Cardinal Wolsey because he had not been able to resolve the issue in the king's favor. A short time later he was stripped of his position as lord chancellor and most of his possessions, including his great estate at Hampton Court. The cardinal was banished to a small castle, and in October 1529 he was accused of treason. Wolsey, who also held the title of archbishop of York, was sent to the northern city, where he lived modestly for a year. In November 1530 he was arrested for high treason and was taken to London for trial and possible execution. When the arresting party was a hundred miles from London, Wolsey fell ill and died.

Anne Boleyn, who had disliked him, celebrated by attending a play, *Of the Cardinal's Going to Hell,* with her friends.

Meanwhile, Catherine and Anne continued to live in different quarters of the same royal residences. After Wolsey's downfall, the king had acquired York Place, his former adviser's London palace, which Henry decided to develop into a complex where he and Anne could live away from the queen. The resulting development also became a center for government in London, later acquiring the name of Whitehall.

Three years had passed since the beginning of the romance between the king and the lady-in-waiting, and yet a decision permitting them to marry had not been reached. Henry had begun to openly show affection toward Anne. He gave her jewelry, expensive clothing, and luxurious furnishings. Some courtiers began to adjust to her presence and power in the court; others were critical. Outside the court, however, Catherine, whose health and spirits were failing, still held the affection of the people.

5 Henry Defines the Church, 1530–1535

The downfall and death of Cardinal Wolsey created a void in the court, which for so many years had been dominated by his strong personality and leadership skills. The remaining eighteen years of Henry's reign would be influenced by the strong will of the king himself.

Biographer N. Brysson Morrison writes:

> With Wolsey went spectacle and the spectacular, with the King came government and rule. The difference between the two men was the difference between personality and character: the King was what Wolsey was not, a realist. . . . He was learning to master himself, to curb a temper that could have betrayed a lesser man into bouts of violence. His passions were strong but he kept them well bridled, his manners were invariably good even under the most trying circumstances, and above all he knew how to keep himself to himself. [22]

NEW LEADERS REPLACE WOLSEY

Without the assistance of his chief adviser, Henry had a greater workload, and the stress began to take its toll on his health. He suffered from headaches, sore throats, and hoarseness, and he had a chronic inflammation of a varicose vein on his thigh.

Henry, however, found taking a more direct hand in government empowering. He attended to governing with great attention to detail. Author Alison Weir writes, "He also paid greater attention to paperwork: Erasmus noted in 1529 that the King personally corrected and amended his letters, often drafting up to four versions before he was satisfied." [23]

Wolsey's death created opportunities for the king's advisers to rise in power. The most important of these was the appointment of Sir Thomas More to replace Wolsey as lord chancellor. More, a scholar, a writer, and a philosopher, was one of the most distinguished men of the time. He had come to Henry's notice in 1515 when he accompanied a delegation to Flanders to settle problems in the wool trade, and he accompanied the king to the Field of the Cloth of Gold in 1520. In 1521 Henry had dubbed More a knight. A lawyer and member of Parliament, More did not represent the church as Wolsey had. He disapproved of annulling the king's marriage, but before his appointment Henry had assured him

A distinguished scholar, writer, and philosopher, Sir Thomas More replaced Thomas Wolsey as Henry's lord chancellor.

that he would not be asked to support the annulment proceedings.

More was also opposed to the Lutheran ideas spreading throughout Europe, and he vowed to treat heretics harshly. During the time he was chancellor, six heretics were burned at the stake.

In fall 1530 Henry appointed Thomas Cromwell, a lawyer who had been an aide to Wolsey, to his council. After the cardinal's death, he rose in power after Cromwell advised Henry to get Parliament's consent to declare himself the head of the church in England. Cromwell, acting as chief secular

minister, prepared a document protesting the fact that the church made laws that were separate from the laws of the kingdom.

Other major appointments included Charles Brandon, the Duke of Suffolk, and the Duke of Norfolk, Anne Boleyn's uncle, who were made joint presidents of the council.

In spite of the pressures of this period, Henry was both artistically and intellectually creative. He composed music, including two choral compositions called motets, which are still part of the church music of England. As a patron of the arts, he commissioned artists and craftsmen to decorate public buildings and palaces, and he endowed colleges and universities.

HENRY EXPANDS THE ROLE OF PARLIAMENT

One of Henry's major accomplishments is his use of Parliament as a tool to enact change. Historically the governing body had met rarely, but when Henry took greater charge, it met more frequently and came to be known as the Reformation Parliament. The membership of Parliament was made up of upper- and middle-class landowners and merchants, many of whom objected to the corruption of the church, which was often more political than spiritual in its actions. Unlike the officials of the church, they were more sympathetic to Henry's problems and were therefore more willing to pass laws to help him accomplish his goals.

One of the ways that Henry used Parliament was to pass statutes that made the clergy subject to the king in spiritual matters. This meant bishops would be chosen by the Crown, not the pope, and when the new bishops were consecrated, the fees that had gone to Rome would no longer be paid. The changes paved the way for the government to assume power over religion, making the church subject to the authority of the state. Henry protested to Parliament that the clergy of England were only partly loyal to him because they also had taken an oath to be faithful to the pope, an action that the king deemed treasonous. The clergy bowed down to the threats of treason, which was punishable by execution, and in May 1532 agreed that church laws had to be approved by the king. The action, called "Submission of the Clergy," caused Thomas More to resign his position as lord chancellor.

Along with these actions, Parliament also declared that they and the king still accepted the Catholic faith, but that their quarrel was with allowing a foreign pope to determine English political affairs.

During this time Anne's power was growing at court, and often she acted as though she, not Catherine, was the queen. Henry continued to give her many lavish gifts, including furs, fine linen for her undergarments, velvet and satin for elegant gowns, and many pieces of jewelry. Among

SIR THOMAS MORE

Sir Thomas More was one of the most respected of Henry VIII's advisers. In the notes for his play, *A Man for All Seasons,* playwright Robert Bolt describes More as a man in his late forties, pale, and medium size. More was born in London in 1478, the son of a prominent judge. After studying at Oxford and becoming a lawyer, he also thought of becoming a monk. Civil service and the desire to serve his country, however, called him. In 1515 Henry sent More with a delegation to Flanders to settle disputes with the wool trade. He also accompanied Henry to the Field of the Cloth of Gold in 1520. Henry made him a knight in 1521.

More helped Henry write his book *Defense of the Seven Sacraments,* in which he answered Martin Luther's complaints against the Catholic Church. After the fall of Cardinal Wolsey, More became lord chancellor. However, he disagreed with Henry's desire to annul his marriage to Queen Catherine, and he resigned his position citing ill health. The real reason was probably because he did not agree with the formation of the new Church of England. When as a matter of conscience he refused to swear to the Act of Succession and the Act of Supremacy, he was imprisoned at the Tower of London. He was found guilty of treason and was beheaded on July 6, 1535. He was declared a saint by Pope Pius XI in 1935.

Samuel Johnson, one of England's most famous writers, wrote of More, "He was the person of the greatest virtue that these islands ever produced."

the jewels were a ring set with nineteen small diamonds and twenty-one rubies, and a bracelet set with a miniature portrait of Henry.

ANNE'S RELIGIOUS VIEWS CAUSE CONCERN

Although Anne was high tempered and flirtatious, she was also an intelligent and widely read woman, whose studies led her to favor religious reforms that were dangerously close to the Protestant views of Luther. Among these were the concepts that people could interpret the Bible for themselves and that it should be read in English rather than in Latin, ideas that were considered heresy. These radical viewpoints concerned traditionalists in the court, many of whom also disliked her arrogant behavior.

Because she supported religious reform, Anne made several enemies at court, including Eustache Chapuys, the Spanish ambassador to the English court who had allied himself with Queen Catherine. In his

Anne Boleyn was a highly educated and intelligent woman. The fact that she favored religious reform won her several powerful enemies at court.

reports to his superior, Emperor Charles, Chapuys wrote that Anne was a cause of spreading Protestant ideas in England.

In spite of the opposition, however, the Boleyns' power was growing at court. Anne's father was made Earl of Wiltshire and Ormonde. At the banquet given by Henry to celebrate the appointment, Catherine did not attend, and Anne sat in the queen's chair. Anne was also treated with more respect than the Duchess of Suffolk, Henry's sister Mary, who had been queen of France.

CATHERINE IS EJECTED FROM THE COURT

In July 1532 Henry saw Catherine for the last time when he left Windsor at dawn to go hunting with Anne. Earlier that year he had continued trying to convince Catherine to end their marriage, and he had sent Anne's uncle, the Duke of Norfolk, to ask her to submit to the king's demands. Catherine rejected all his arguments. Henry then sent the Duke of Norfolk and a large delegation of nobles to ask the queen if she would agree to accept a decision of a court that would meet away from Rome. Again she insisted that only the pope had the authority to end her marriage.

Following Henry's departure, Catherine was ordered to move, with her household of two hundred people, to the More, one of Wolsey's former homes in Hertfordshire. She was not permitted to stay long at the More, and she was finally taken to an estate in the country, where she remained for two years. As punishment for not agreeing to the annulment, she was forbidden to see her daughter.

Many of the English common people remained critical of Anne Boleyn. To raise her status, Henry gave her the title of Marquess of Pembroke, a position that provided her with a pension of one thousand pounds a year. Her emblem, a lover's knot, which combined her initials with Henry's, began to appear on royal architecture, including Cardinal's College, founded by Wolsey at Oxford, which later became known as King's College. The king ordered Catherine to give up her royal jewels for Anne's use, and a trip was planned for Henry and his lover to go to France to meet Francis I. The recognition of another monarch would be an official acknowledgment of her position as the future queen. The trip in October 1532 was successful.

ANNE AND HENRY MARRY

Sometime before the end of the year Anne became Henry's mistress, and in December or early January she became pregnant. Marriage between Henry and Anne was now an urgent issue because the child would have to be considered legitimate in order to be heir to the throne. Around late January 1533 the two were married in a secret ceremony. Only her immediate family, two close friends, and the priest attended. The secrecy was necessary because Henry was still legally married to Catherine. Actions to sever his first marriage moved forward.

After the death of William Warham, the archbishop of Canterbury who had not favored the annulment, Henry had pushed

HENRY'S PETS

Henry VIII was very fond of animals, and he had many pets. In Henry VIII: The King and His Court, *author Alison Weir writes about Henry's menagerie.*

Henry VIII kept canaries and nightingales in ornamental bird-cages hanging in the windows at Hampton Court. He also kept ferrets, although he forbade courtiers to do so.

Henry's favorite pets were his dogs, especially beagles, spaniels, and greyhounds; the latter were considered a particularly noble breed. Over the years the King sent hundreds of such dogs, all "garnished with a good iron collar," as gifts to the Holy Roman Emperor and the King of France. Henry's own dogs wore decorative collars of velvet—permitted only to royal dogs—and kid [soft leather], with or without torettes [spikes] of silver and gold; some were adorned with pearls or the King's arms and . . . rose badges. His dogs' coats were of white silk, and the dogs had their fur regularly rubbed down with "hair cloth." Sixty-five dog leashes were found in Henry's closets after his death. Pet dogs were fed bread, not meat, to discourage them from developing hunting instincts. Two of Henry's dogs, Cut and Ball, were prone to getting lost, and he paid out the huge sum of nearly 15s [about £225 today] in rewards to those who brought them back.

for the appointment of Anne Boleyn's former chaplain, Thomas Cranmer, whom he thought he could control. In March 1533 Pope Clement VII consecrated Cranmer as archbishop of Canterbury, and Henry applied pressure to Parliament to pass the Act in Restraint of Appeals, which ruled that all spiritual matters would from that time on be judged in England instead of Rome. The archbishop of Canterbury would be the final arbiter in any judgment. This ruling meant that Catherine could not appeal her side to Rome. It also made Princess Mary illegitimate.

On April 9, 1533, a delegation broke the news of Henry's and Anne's marriage to Catherine, telling her that she was no longer queen but would now be known as Princess Dowager. Neither the king nor Catherine attended the divorce hearings, and Henry busied himself arranging for Anne's coronation.

ANNE IS CROWNED QUEEN OF ENGLAND

On May 23, 1533, Archbishop Cranmer announced that the marriage between the king and Catherine was invalid, thus permitting a divorce. A week later on June 1, he presided over celebrations for the coronation of Anne as queen.

The ceremonies had begun on May 29 when Anne left Greenwich and arrived by boat at the Tower of London. She wore a gown of golden cloth and was escorted by fifty decorated barges representing the guilds of London. Cannons were fired in celebration. Arriving at the Tower of London, Anne was met by Henry, who kissed her.

The next day, people thronged the streets of London to see the royal procession wend its way through the city. The event was filled with the pageantry typical of the time. Anne wore her long black hair loose in the style of a bride, and she carried a bouquet of flowers. Her crimson brocade dress was embellished with precious stones, and over it she wore a purple velvet robe. She rode in a litter at the head of a large group of nobles and attendants. Along the way the procession stopped to view pageants and dramatic spectacles. At one of the stops, a city official stepped forward and gave Anne a purse filled with a thousand marks in gold. Although it was the custom to give such a gift to a new queen, she was expected to return it so it could be distributed among the officials. It was noticed by many that the new queen kept the money for herself, a move that reinforced the public's negative

Anne Boleyn rides at the center of a procession making its way through the streets of London during her coronation ceremony in 1533.

opinion of her. Criticism, however, had never bothered Anne, who exclaimed, "Let who will, complain."[24]

The next morning Anne, accompanied by nobles, was crowned queen in Westminster Abbey. Henry, following the tradition that a king did not attend a coronation that was separate from his own, was not at the ceremony.

ANNE REMAINS UNPOPULAR WITH THE PEOPLE

In spite of the celebrations and the free wine that flowed for all, the people of London were not enthusiastic about their new queen. In private they referred to her as a whore and a harlot. Henry, however, was elated with the way things had turned out. Author Carolly Erickson writes: "For better or worse he had taken his destiny into his own hands, ending the unendurable cycle of false hopes, fresh starts, and endless delays in Rome. He had made the woman he loved his queen, and within months the greatest desire of his adult life would be fulfilled. His queen would bear his son."[25]

Not long after the coronation, rumors began to circulate that Anne and Henry were fighting over his flirtations with ladies of the court. Anne, who had a temper, was jealous of Henry's infidelities, which Catherine had overlooked.

On July 11, 1533, Pope Clement VII excommunicated Henry from the Catholic Church, declaring that any child of Anne's would be illegitimate.

THE BIRTH OF PRINCESS ELIZABETH

As the summer drew to a close, Henry rejoiced in the idea that Anne would soon give birth to his son and heir, as was predicted by the royal doctors and astrologers. Henry ordered preparations for a tournament to celebrate the birth. The male baby would be named Edward or Henry.

Anne retired from the court on August 26 to prepare for the baby's birth, and on September 7, 1533, she gave birth to a healthy baby girl, who was named Elizabeth in honor of Henry's mother. The infant princess was also given the title of Princess of Wales, the title that Mary had held, and Henry's oldest child was ordered to call her new sister princess, an order that she refused.

Henry was very disappointed that the baby was not a boy, but he did order that masses be sung in thanksgiving for the successful birth. Although she was christened with royal pomp, her father did not attend the ceremony, and he canceled the tournaments that had been planned to celebrate the birth of a son.

THE ACT OF SUCCESSION AND THE CHURCH OF ENGLAND

The lengthy arguments about Henry's annulment had convinced him that he should take control over the church. He was supported in this by his adviser, Thomas Cromwell, who by 1534 had become the principal royal secretary. Cromwell was firm in his hatred for the clergy, and he be-

THE REFORMATION

The Reformation was the religious movement that led to Protestantism. It began in 1517 when a German monk and professor of theology, Martin Luther, nailed a list of ninety-five objections to the policies of the Catholic Church on the door of the church in Wittenburg, Germany. One of the abuses was the sale of indulgences, or pardons for sins. Luther believed that a person could only be saved by a belief in Christ. Luther was excommunicated from the Catholic Church, and when he refused to give up his beliefs, he was declared an outlaw who could be killed without penalties. Nevertheless, his ideas spread throughout northern Europe and crossed into England where they were considered heresies.

The movement also had political and economic causes. By the sixteenth century, the power of the European kings had increased, and cities were beginning to replace a largely rural and agricultural society. The invention of moveable type led to printing of books, which became increasingly available to people outside the clergy. As people read about the new ideas, some were attracted to them. By the end of the sixteenth century, Protestantism was established in almost half of Europe.

Although he broke with the Catholic Church, Henry VIII remained essentially Catholic in his religious beliefs. Protestant ideas advanced during the reign of his son Edward. When Henry's daughter, Mary I, became queen, she suppressed and persecuted Protestants and restored Catholicism as the state religion. Under Elizabeth I, a more moderate form of Protestantism called Anglicanism became the rule under the Church of England, where it continues as the state religion today. The Episcopal Church in the United States is a branch of the Anglican faith.

lieved that the church needed to be reformed. He convinced Henry that in England the church should be free of the control of the pope in Rome and that the king should be the head of the church. Henry was also encouraged by Anne, who was interested in the new Protestant ideas circulating throughout Europe. Even before their marriage she had read William Tyndale's *The Obedience of a Christian Man,* a book which attacked the power of the pope.

Henry used Parliament to enact laws giving more power to the monarch in church matters. In 1533 the Act in Restraint of Appeals, which had been passed by Parliament, required that all future bishops and archbishops be appointed by the king. Dispensations and rules would be determined in Canterbury, not Rome. In 1534 Parliament went even further by passing the Act of Supremacy, which recognized the king as the supreme head of the church in England. The act gave Henry the power of the pope in England and created the Church of England. All ties with the Roman Catholic Church were severed.

At the same time Parliament passed the Act of Succession, which formally declared the validity of Henry and Anne's marriage and their children's right to rule England. The title of princess was taken from Mary, who was now referred to as Lady Mary. The people of England were required to swear to the new rule, which denied the authority of the pope. Those who refused to take the oath were considered traitors.

TORTURE AND EXECUTIONS

A violent period followed. Many priests and monks did swear to the new rules but others refused. Those who resisted were tortured, and some were killed by being drawn and quartered while still alive. Others were hanged or burned to death. Catherine and Mary refused to take the oath, but because of their status they were

In 1534 Parliament passed the Act of Supremacy that recognized the king as the supreme head of the Church of England and severed all ties with the Catholic Church.

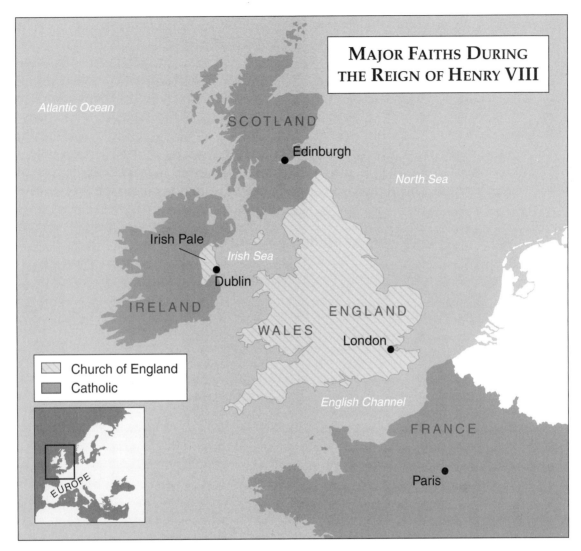

Atlantic Ocean

SCOTLAND

Edinburgh

North Sea

Irish Pale

Irish Sea

Dublin

IRELAND

ENGLAND

WALES

London

Church of England

Catholic

English Channel

EUROPE

FRANCE

Paris

spared. Henry feared that executing the former queen or imprisoning her in the Tower of London would inflame his subjects, who still held her in high esteem. By now Catherine's health had failed, and she was not expected to live for long.

Both Henry's former friend and adviser, Sir Thomas More, and Catherine's advocate, Bishop John Fisher, refused to take the oath and were arrested. Fisher, who believed that the king could never take the place of the pope, was made a cardinal of the Catholic Church during his imprisonment in the Tower of London, but this did not spare his life. He was executed in June 1535. More refused to sign any document that denied the pope's authority. He spent a year in the Tower of London, and on July 6, 1535, he was beheaded, saying that although he was the king's loyal servant, he served God first. The execution of the prominent bishop and famous scholar shocked people both in England and in Europe and brought criticism from Erasmus and Emperor Charles.

Throughout England, neighbor denounced neighbor, and many were fearful of voicing their opinions about the king and queen. Cromwell actively evaluated reports of criticism against the monarchy, and many people were executed for treason. He also confiscated the lands and wealth of the Catholic monasteries, giving them to the Crown, a move that also shocked many.

Henry, who had once been loyal to the pope, was now defiantly asserting his unlimited power, and his huge ego made him insensitive to criticism. Now in his forties, he had developed the inner conviction that he was right before God and Parliament. Among his jewelry, he had a bracelet that bore the inscription, "to die rather than change my mind."[26] In the future he would follow his own instincts and rely less on the advice of others.

6 To Arouse the King's Anger Means Death, 1535–1540

By 1535 Henry had become a feared monarch, and those who crossed him were often met with death. He was unable to accept any viewpoint other than his own. Biographer N. Brysson Morrison writes: "Henry was accustomed to everyone, archbishop and bishop included, prostrating themselves at his feet. . . . It was now second nature for him to believe not only that he could do no wrong but that everything he did was right."[27]

HENRY LOSES INTEREST IN ANNE

The happiness that Henry enjoyed in his relations with Anne before their marriage began to wither after the birth of Princess Elizabeth. In early 1534 Anne had become pregnant a second time, and a silver cradle was ordered for the new baby. Unfortunately Anne miscarried, but she soon became pregnant again. After that pregnancy also ended in miscarriage, an element of distrust entered the marriage. Anne was now in her mid-thirties, and was beginning to show her age. Henry had already found new, younger favorites in the court, and he was especially attracted to Jane Seymour, a gentle lady-in-waiting. After only two years of marriage, he began to regret his decision to marry Anne.

Anne knew that Henry would only be happy if she bore him a son. Her problems were compounded by her continued unpopularity among the people, who held her partly responsible for the bloodshed that was rampant in England as a result of the religious reforms. In frustration, she turned her anger against Henry's other daughter, Mary, around whom some of Anne's critics had rallied.

THE FORMER QUEEN DIES

By the summer of 1535 Henry's first wife had been moved to the rundown Kimbolton Castle, where she lived in seclusion. Most of Catherine's possessions as queen had been taken from her, and as a punishment for her obstinance she was not allowed to see her daughter. Her household consisted of only three women attendants who cooked and tasted her food as there was a fear that she might be poisoned. Her only other visitors were her priest and her doctor. Her health continued to fail, and by December she was near death.

THE PALACES OF HENRY VIII

Greenwich Palace and Hampton Court played major roles during the life of Henry VIII. Both were located on the Thames River, which was a thoroughfare for royal travel. Many important events took place at Greenwich Palace. Henry loved it because it was his birthplace and he had spent most of his boyhood there or at nearby Eltham Palace, where he was first introduced to Erasmus by Thomas More. During the first half of his reign, he spent more time at Greenwich than at any of his other palaces. The palace included a large park where he could hunt, and he enjoyed watching his ships being built at the nearby shipyard. Henry and Catherine of Aragon were married at Greenwich, and it was from there that Anne Boleyn sailed down the Thames to be crowned queen. Henry's son Edward was born at Greenwich, and it was there that his favorite queen, Jane Seymour, died.

Henry made many improvements to the palace during the 1530s. His bedroom, library, and study were probably in the great tower. Stables and a new tiltyard with viewing towers and gallery satisfied his interests in horsemanship and jousting. The chapel was rebuilt, and the queen's rooms were refurbished. The palace was demolished in 1662, and today little remains.

Hampton Court, on the other hand, remains as a good example of Tudor architecture and engineering. Confiscated from Cardinal Wolsey, the palace was also the home of Henry VIII. Wolsey and Henry built an efficient system of pipes and drains that remained in use until 1871. The system brought water to the bathrooms of the king and queen and also served the rest of the palace. At Hampton Court, Henry installed a famous astronomical clock, which was designed by Nicolaus Kratzer. The clock shows the hours, month, date, phases of the moon, the movement of the constellations in the zodiac, and the time of high water at London Bridge. A sundial, which shows the hour, month, sign of the moon, and the tides, was installed in 1540.

The morning of January 7, 1536, the day she died, Catherine wrote a letter to Henry in which she greeted him as her lord and king and forgave him for his actions against her. She also begged him to be kind to their daughter. The letter was signed, "Catherine, Queen of England."

When Henry learned of her death, he cried, but then he and Anne dressed in yellow satin clothing rather than in black, as though they were rejoicing. The mood in court was one of triumph rather than grief. Anne was pregnant again, but on the day of Catherine's funeral she suffered a miscarriage. Henry told one of his friends that he believed he had been lured into marriage with Anne by witchcraft and considered it invalid. He believed that God was against the marriage and would not permit them to have a son.

HENRY MOVES AGAINST ANNE

By February 1536 Henry had left Greenwich and Anne had moved to another royal residence, York Place. He returned to Greenwich from time to time to court Jane Seymour, and in March, he appointed Jane's brother, Sir Edward Seymour, to a high court position. The Seymours, who disliked Anne and were conspiring against her, advised Jane to refuse Henry's advances in order to improve her chances for a royal marriage. In March the king sent her a gift of gold coins, which she returned, an action which impressed Henry.

Jane came from a noble and prominent family. Her father, Sir John Seymour, was a knight who had been close to Henry for many years. Her mother, Margery Wentworth, was a descendant of King Edward III and was Henry's fifth cousin. Jane herself was not a beauty, but she was distinguished by her chastity and sweet personality. Unlike Anne Boleyn, whose dark complexion and fiery temper went against the standards of beauty and behavior of the time, Jane's pale blue eyes, light blonde hair, and modesty personified the English ideas of beauty and femininity in the sixteenth century.

After her failed pregnancy, Anne began to indulge herself by spending large sums of money on clothing for herself and for her daughter. Behind the scenes, those who did not like the queen, including Thomas Cromwell, were promoting Jane Seymour.

There were personal and political reasons for Cromwell's position. First, it was important to smooth relations between England and Spain. The feelings of Emperor Charles had to be calmed after Henry's in-sulting behavior toward his aunt, the late queen. Cromwell also knew that his survival as chief adviser to the king depended on providing him with the wife he desired.

Anne watched her power slip away. The first move was made on April 23, when an appointment to the prestigious Order of the Garter, an elite club made up of royals and nobles, went to Sir Nicholas Carew rather than to her brother George Boleyn. The next

Henry began courting Jane Seymour in early 1536. She became queen after Anne was executed.

day, Cromwell prompted the king to sign a document to investigate Anne's activities that might lead to the charge of treason. On April 30 Mark Smeaton, a musician at the court who was a friend of Anne's, was arrested and tortured at the Tower of London until he confessed to adultery with the queen.

The following day a splendid tournament was scheduled to celebrate May Day, and Anne and Henry attended together. The principal challenger was the queen's brother who faced Sir Henry Norris, a friend of both of the royals. When Anne dropped her handkerchief at the feet of Norris, he picked it up and kissed it. Henry, who suspected that there was a relationship between the queen and Norris, became angry, and with six of his friends got up and left.

ARRESTS ARE MADE

Within a few days Anne's brother, George Boleyn, and Norris were arrested along with another handsome courtier, Sir Francis Weston, and all were charged with adultery with Anne, an accusation that was based on Smeaton's testimony. The charge was also that of treason against the king. Anne, too, was soon arrested and taken by barge to the Tower of London, where she was imprisoned in the same rooms she had stayed in before her coronation. Among the twenty-two charges against her was the charge of incest with her brother—an accusation made to blacken her name. She was also accused of trying to poison the king, Catherine, and Mary.

Author Alison Weir writes:

Most modern historians are of the opinion that Anne was not guilty of any of the twenty-two charges of adultery laid against her; eleven of them can be proved false. . . . The circumstances of her fall suggest strongly that she was framed. . . . However, her reputation, her flirtatious nature, her enjoyment of male company, and her indulgence in the amorous banter and interplay of courtly love all made the charges against her believable. Not only the King but many other people thought her guilty. [28]

Anne Boleyn was accused of treason and lesser charges and imprisoned in the Tower of London.

Thousands of spectators watch as those Henry VIII accused of treason in 1536 are beheaded near the Tower of London.

The Accused Are Executed

Fear spread throughout the court as several more men were arrested. During this time Henry kept a low profile, and Jane Seymour was taken to lodgings near Hampton Court, where the king could quietly visit her by boat. His mood was happy, and during the evenings, he partied with ladies of the court on his barge.

On May 12 four of the accused men were sentenced to death by being cut down while alive, disemboweled, castrated, and finally having their limbs quartered. On May 17 the accused men were executed at the Tower of London by beheading, their

sentences reduced from the cruel death to which they had been condemned. All swore loyalty to the king before they died.

The queen and her brother were tried by a jury of their peers three days later in the Great Hall of the Tower of London. It was estimated that two thousand spectators viewed the trial, which was presided over by the Duke of Norfolk, uncle of the accused. Anne was tried first, and she swore that she was innocent. Both the queen and her brother were sentenced to die by beheading or burning, whichever the king chose.

During her two remaining days, Anne's behavior alternated between hysteria and calm. For her execution, Anne wore a loose, dark gray gown, a red petticoat, and an ermine cloak. Her long hair was held up by a white linen cap. Before she died, she asked permission to speak, saying she accepted the judgment against her and asked the king's blessing. She then knelt, was blindfolded, and was beheaded with one stroke of the executioner's sharp sword. Her severed head and body were buried at the Chapel of St. Peter ad Vincula on the grounds of the Tower of London.

During the years of Henry's courtship and their marriage, Anne had been one of the most important women in Europe, but her rapid descent from power is a sign of the perils that came with high position during Henry's reign. The purpose of her death was to clear the way for Henry to get a new wife. On receiving the news of Anne's death, Henry went to visit Jane Seymour.

HENRY MARRIES JANE

Henry lost no time in proposing to Jane Seymour the day after Anne's execution. The secret engagement took place at Hampton Court on May 20, 1536, after Bishop Cranmer had issued a dispensation because the two were distantly related. Their quiet marriage took place ten days later on May 30.

Henry was delighted with his new wife and gave her gifts that emphasized her new status. One was a magnificent pendant of emeralds and pearls designed by the artist Hans Holbein. Another gift, a heavy gold cup, was engraved with Jane's motto "Bound to obey and serve."

Jane was a traditionalist who demanded that her ladies-in-waiting behave properly and dress modestly. A good Catholic, she

hoped for the return of Roman Catholicism to England. Those who supported her beliefs encouraged her to befriend Princess Mary, who was still out of favor with Henry because she, as a Catholic, had refused to agree to the Act of Supremacy, which made Henry the supreme head of the Church of England. Mary also rejected the Act of Succession, which removed her as the primary heir to the throne.

Eustache Chapuys, the Spanish ambassador, was among those who hoped to see Catholicism restored in England. He visited Mary, now twenty years old, and advised her to submit to the king. As the representative of her mother's nephew, King Charles of Spain, he knew that his king would not be content until Mary's position in the English court was restored. He also feared that if she did not submit, she might be killed. Mary replied that she had already written to Henry congratulating him on his recent wedding. When Henry did not respond to her overture for reconciliation, she wrote to Cromwell for assistance, saying she had done all that her conscience would allow. Cromwell sent a group of deputies to hear her swear to the Act of Supremacy. When she failed to agree that her own birth was illegitimate, she received a stern letter from Cromwell ordering her to sign an enclosed statement acknowledging Henry as sovereign and agreeing to accept all the laws of the land. If she refused, she would face possible imprisonment and execution. In light of these threats she finally agreed to sign a statement acknowledging Henry as supreme sovereign and her parents' marriage unlawful. Henry then ordered that she repeat the statement of submission in front of his council. Her household was then reestablished, and she spent Christmas at Greenwich Palace.

A NEW ORDER OF SUCCESSION

In June 1536 Parliament passed a new order of succession, which gave the heirs between Henry and Jane the right to inherit the throne, and gave the king the right to nominate those who would rule after his death if his children were minors. The new order meant that both princesses, Mary and Elizabeth, were considered illegitimate. Only the king could decide whether to acknowledge them as his legitimate children.

REBELLION IN THE NORTH

While Jane and Henry enjoyed life at court during the summer of 1536, unrest spread throughout much of England. Many people resented the changes in the church and wanted a return to their old religion. They were particularly disturbed by the tearing down of monasteries by the king's commissioners. Hostility was strongest in the north of England, where the people especially resented Cromwell's strict taxes and Cranmer's religious reforms.

The hostilities resulted in uprisings and rebellions that started in Lincolnshire and spread throughout the north. Thirty thousand

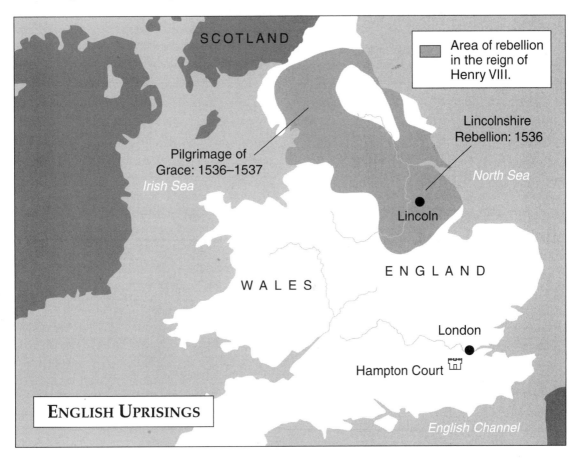

men marched in defense of the Catholic Church in what came to be known as the Pilgrimage of Grace.

Henry was appalled at the rebellion, but he sent the Duke of Norfolk to meet with its leaders, especially a lawyer named Robert Aske. Norfolk told Aske that the king would pardon the rebels if they would make their specific demands to him. He would visit the north, and Jane's coronation as queen would take place in the north at York. Based on these promises Aske told his troops to go home, and a truce was declared.

Henry Breaks His Promises

In January 1537 Henry was overjoyed to discover that Jane was pregnant, but he soon betrayed her by breaking his pledge to the leaders of the rebellion. Near the beginning of the rebellions she had begged him to reestablish the abbeys, but he had angrily refused, telling her that she should not meddle in his affairs, reminding her of the fate of her predecessor. When some of the men who had been in the rebellion saw that the king was not planning to consider their demands, they broke the truce.

Henry ordered the leaders of the rebellion arrested, and all were executed—even those who had not participated in the more recent fights. Jane's coronation at York and the king's trip north were both cancelled. Henry could not stand for revolt within England, and he used violence to restore order and resolve one of the greatest challenges of his reign.

Jane Gives Birth to a Son, Prince Edward

In late September Queen Jane retired to her quarters, and on October 9 she went into labor. Her labor was extremely painful and prolonged, lasting thirty hours. Finally on October 12, 1537, she gave birth to a son, who was named Edward. To celebrate, guns

Henry was overjoyed when Jane gave birth to Prince Edward, seen here with the king at age ten.

were fired, bells rang throughout London, and many joyful feasts were held.

Jane participated in her son's christening and baptism three days later, but a short time afterward she became very ill. Twelve days after Edward's birth she died, having been given the last rites of the Catholic Church.

Henry was heartbroken and went into seclusion. Jane was the only wife for whom he wore mourning clothing, but not long after her death he began to make inquiries about seeking another wife.

POLITICAL ISSUES DRIVE HENRY'S SEARCH FOR ANOTHER WIFE

Early in 1538 the search for a new wife for the king became serious. Henry was not particularly eager to marry again, but he knew he must do so for two reasons. He needed another son as a backup heir to the throne, and the security of England depended on mending his relationships with Emperor Charles and King Francis. It was feared that the two rulers might unite against England.

Although Cromwell took charge of the search for a new queen, Henry wanted to have his own say in the final selection. Biographer Antonia Fraser writes:

> In 1538 Henry VIII wanted—no, he *expected*—to be diverted, entertained and excited. . . . At the same time the King allowed his ambassadors to proceed in the time-honoured manner with the ritual inspection of suitable candidates, not seeing there might be some innate contradiction between the demands

of diplomacy and those of a romantic but by now deeply self-indulgent nature.[29]

The king, now in his late forties, was not as attractive as he had once been. In Europe his reputation had been tarnished by the execution of Anne Boleyn and his speedy marriage to one of her ladies-in-waiting. Several princesses turned down his offers of marriage, one saying if she had two heads she would gladly offer one to Henry.

RELIGIOUS REFORMS CONTINUE

During this time, Henry and Cromwell continued their campaign to suppress the monasteries and convents, to reinforce the religious changes the king wanted. The suppression also brought more riches for the monarchy. As monasteries and convents were plundered, their treasures and wealth were taken for the king. The looting, however, had serious cultural and social effects. Libraries and priceless manuscripts were destroyed, and many of the hospitals for the poor, which were run by the monasteries, disappeared.

As head of the new Church of England, Henry ordered that a Bible be placed in every church and that priests read from it in English rather than Latin. In his beliefs, however, he was still essentially Catholic, and he rejected most of the Protestant reforms of Martin Luther. The new church retained many of the customs of Roman Catholicism.

Nevertheless, his actions shocked the pope, the Emperor Charles, and King Francis, who negotiated a ten-year truce to resolve their differences and to unite to attack England. Catholic Scotland was also urged to invade England.

In the face of an attack, the English people rallied behind their king and built protective ramparts along the shores. To gain the support of the House of Cleves, German nobles not affiliated with Charles's Holy Roman Empire, Cromwell suggested a marriage between Henry and one of the Duke of Cleves's sisters.

ANNE OF CLEVES

The court artist, Hans Holbein, was sent to paint portraits of the two sisters for Henry's approval. The flattering portrait of Anne was so lovely that Henry agreed to marry her—an unfortunate decision.

Anne of Cleves had been raised in a provincial court where her primary training had been in domestic skills like embroidery. Because she had not been educated in languages other than her own dialect of German, she knew no English. Unlike Henry's other wives she was not musical, an attribute Henry, a gifted musician himself, valued highly. Although little concern was directed to her suitability as wife to the older, more sophisticated Henry, a match was agreed upon and plans were made for her journey to England.

To avoid her capture at sea by the forces of Francis or Charles, it was decided that Anne would travel by land to Calais and then cross the short distance of the English Channel by ship. She arrived in England on New Year's Day 1540. Eager to meet her, Henry and several of his friends had ridden to Rochester where she was staying. When he came into her room unannounced, he was shocked by her appearance, which differed greatly from Holbein's portrait. Her height, dark complexion, and old-fashioned clothing repelled him, and he was also offended by her lack of culture. Unfortunately breaking the marriage contract would insult the House of Cleves, and England needed them as an ally against Charles and Francis.

In spite of his revulsion, Henry treated Anne politely in public and continued the plans for their marriage, which took place on January 6, 1540. The marriage proved short-lived. Henry was miserable and told his close friends that his new wife disgusted him. Anne, however, was unaware of his feelings toward her. Henry instead directed his anger at Cromwell, believing that his chief adviser had tricked him into an unpleasant marriage.

Although Anne presided over the elaborate May Day celebration of 1540, it was her last official act as queen. In July 1540 the marriage was annulled. Anne, who was not given much choice in the matter, accepted the decision and decided to remain in England rather than go back home in disgrace. In return she was given two manor houses and a large pension of twenty-six hundred pounds a year. It was decreed that in the future she would be known as a sister of the king and would have precedence over all other women except the queen and the king's two daughters. Her freedom, however, was somewhat limited, as all further communication with her family had to be approved by the king.

CROMWELL IS ARRESTED

Cromwell's role in the marriage of Henry and Anne of Cleves proved to be his undoing. Different factions constantly vied for

HANS HOLBEIN, COURT PAINTER

Art was very important in the court of Henry VIII. In Henry VIII: A European Court in England, *edited by David Starkey, author Susan Foster writes:*

Henry VIII, like other sixteenth-century European monarchs, needed painters to paint his royal palaces: from simply painting the window frames red to creating elaborate subject paintings and altarpieces. They were also needed to provide banners and heraldry for weddings, funerals and coronations; to paint cloths of honour and royal barges; to design and make stage properties for Court entertainments; to produce designs for the Court goldsmiths to work from; to paint portraits of the royal family as diplomatic presents or as part of marriage negotiations.

The most famous court painter in the court of Henry VIII was Hans Holbein, who left his home town of Basel in Switzerland in 1526 to seek his fortune in England. By 1536 he was referred to as the king's painter. Although he was known in Basel for his woodcuts and his decorative paintings on the exteriors of houses, in England he is most famous for his portraits in oil paint of the king and other important people. His portraits feature psychological depth and detailed accessories. Between 1538 and 1539 he was sent to various courts in Europe to paint portraits of the women who were candidates to become Henry's fourth wife. His complementary portraits of Anne of Cleves delighted Henry. A full-size version is in the Louvre in Paris, and a miniature is in the Victoria and Albert Museum in London. He also painted portraits of Prince Edward, Jane Seymour, Sir Thomas More, and many of the important courtiers. His portraits and drawings of a portly Henry VIII, decked out in the elegant clothing and jewelry he loved, provide modern viewers with the image of the powerful, arrogant king.

Hans Holbein painted portraits of influential figures, including this one of Anne of Cleves, Henry's fourth wife.

During his ten years in the English court, Holbein produced 150 life-size and miniature portraits of royalty and the nobility. Along with the royal goldsmith, he also helped design the royal cradle for Princess Elizabeth and other pieces of gold and silver. Holbein died in London in 1543, probably from the plague.

power in Henry's court, and Cromwell's enemies seized this opportunity. The faction headed by the Duke of Norfolk had opposed the German marriage alliance that had been Cromwell's idea. Behind the scenes, Norfolk was also promoting Henry's romance with Norfolk's nineteen-year-old niece, Catherine Howard. Henry took their side. On June 10 Cromwell was arrested for heresy and treason and was imprisoned at the Tower of London. He was accused of protecting Lutherans and other heretics. Henry, who did not hesitate to eliminate those who displeased him, ignored his former adviser's pleas for mercy. On July 28, 1540, Cromwell was beheaded, and to justify the execution, three Protestants were burned at the stake a short time later.

Henry, now forty-nine years old, was no longer the handsome young monarch who charmed England at his coronation. He had turned into a cruel tyrant who killed those who got in his way.

7 The Final Years, 1540–1547

The final years of Henry's life were marked by ill health, two more marriages, many executions, and continued jockeying to establish England's importance among the powerful nations of Europe. Henry enjoyed his role as supreme leader of the new Church of England, but many of his subjects did not accept the establishment of the new religion. Those eager to promote the new church struggled against the heretical ideas of the Protestant Reformation and the powerful factions who plotted for the reestablishment of Roman Catholicism, causing instability in Henry's court. When the king married Catherine Howard in the summer of 1540, however, he was optimistic about his future.

Henry's and Catherine Howard's marriage was one of opposites. Now forty-nine, Henry was no longer a handsome man, and he suffered from bouts of illness caused by a chronic ulcer in his leg. His huge appetite for meat washed down with beer and wine had caused him to become very fat. According to measurements for an armor made for him in 1540, he had a fifty-four-inch waist and a fifty-seven-inch chest. His bride, Catherine Howard, was a slender, attractive teenager, nearly thirty years younger than the king.

CATHERINE HOWARD

Although she was not from a wealthy branch of the family, the Howards, headed by the powerful Duke of Norfolk, was one of the most powerful in England. After her mother's death, Catherine had been brought up with cousins in the household of the Dowager Duchess of Norfolk. As he had done for her cousin, Anne Boleyn, her uncle, the Duke of Norfolk, contrived to introduce Catherine at court as a lady-in-waiting to the current queen, in hopes that she might make a match that would be advantageous both to her and her family.

The Howards were a Catholic family that had seen its power diminish with the rise of the Church of England. When the duke and his allies noticed that Henry was attracted to Catherine, they began to use her as a pawn to improve their position at court and restore Catholicism to England.

Henry was madly in love with his young bride and ordered many banquets and hunts to celebrate the marriage. He also showered her with many expensive gifts of jewelry and fine clothing. For New Year's 1541, he gave her a necklace of six diamonds, five rubies, and pearls, and a black velvet muffler trimmed with sable fur and

Catherine Howard was nearly thirty years younger than Henry when they married in 1540.

pearls. She was also given manors and castles, and her family members were granted high positions in the court.

Catherine, an impressionable girl, was captivated by the king's power and lavish gifts. Author Antonia Fraser writes:

> Such a level of naivety, such a belief in his omnipotence, made it easy for Queen Katherine to regard King Henry with bedazzled reverence; and then there was

gratitude for his generosity. . . . At the same time, the experience of reverence and gratitude did not mean that Katherine Howard had radically changed her character when she became Queen. [30]

Although Catherine was inexperienced in dealing with power, she was not innocent in the ways of love. While living in the home of the Dowager Duchess of Norfolk, she had sexual relations with Francis Dereham, a young noble who was also part of the household. Before she came to the court, the two had talked of getting married.

In spring 1541 Henry became seriously ill with severe pain in his leg and high fever. His mood became savage, and feeling sorry for himself, he vented his anger on anyone who crossed his will. Catherine was forbidden to come into his rooms because he did not want her to see him as an invalid. Some historians believe that during this time, she began to draw her attention to some of the young men in the court.

A Season of Bloodshed

In the summer of 1541, once he fully recovered from his illness, Henry planned a state visit to the north of England to inspect distant parts of the country he had never seen. The trip involved traveling with a large party, including five thousand nobles, servants, advisers, knights, archers, and his new queen. The party would be away from London for several months, so to avoid any threat of rebellion in his absence, Henry ordered the execution of a number of noble prisoners held in the Tower of London. One was the elderly countess Margaret

Pole, the mother of several nobles who were possible challengers to the throne. Her gory beheading by an inexperienced executioner caused shock throughout the country, and many people secretly were critical of the king.

Henry seemed to enjoy his power over life and death, and he did not hesitate in ordering executions, sometimes offering forgiveness at the last minute. Although his conscience did not seem to bother him, the violence hurt his reputation both at home and in Europe.

THE TRIP NORTH

Henry wanted to impress the people in the north of England, especially those of York, which had been a center of rebellion for years. The area included supporters for the Plantagenet faction, which had fought against Tudors for the throne of England during the Wars of the Roses before Henry's birth. He also arranged to meet with his nephew James V, king of Scotland, in York, with whom he was at times at war.

PRINCE EDWARD

While Henry was fretting over the infidelities of Catherine Howard, he was also worried about his four-year-old son's health. When the royals returned to London from the north, they learned that the young child had suffered from a high fever, and his life was in danger. Although he recovered from the illness, it damaged his health, causing him to be frail. Portraits of the young prince show him to be a handsome, slender child.

In her book *The Private Life of Henry VIII*, author N. Brysson Morrison writes about Edward:

> Highly intelligent, like all Henry's children, from the beginning he took the liveliest interest in all that was going on around him. He was a scholarly boy who played the lute, was thrilled by the stars, and learnt Latin, Greek, French and Italian. Beloved by his father's people, they called him England's Treasure.

When his father died in 1547, Edward was only ten years old, and although he was named king, others took charge of the decisions a monarch might make. The first regent was Edward's uncle, the Duke of Somerset, brother of his mother, Jane Seymour. The duke acted as king in all but name. Later he was displaced by the Duke of Northumberland. In 1553, when the young king was near death, Northumberland convinced him to alter the succession in favor of the duke's granddaughter, Lady Jane Grey, great-niece of Henry VIII. Lady Jane ruled briefly as queen, but gave up the throne to Mary, who, to solidify her position, had Jane beheaded.

When the trip began, Henry and Catherine seemed somewhat distant from one another. Henry was frustrated that after almost a year of marriage Catherine had not yet become pregnant.

When they finally arrived at York, the men who had rebelled against him five years earlier during the northern uprisings knelt before him to ask his forgiveness. Despite this, Henry was disappointed that his nephew James decided to stay in Scotland rather than meet and risk being captured by the English. To make matters worse, the Scots were sending raiding parties across the border to attack English settlements, which infuriated Henry. He ordered his men to retaliate with vengeance.

When the royals returned to Hampton Court in late October, Henry was faced with the bad news that his son, Prince Edward, was very ill with a fever and was in danger of dying. Not long after, Henry received the equally troubling news that the queen had been unfaithful to him.

A ROYAL SCANDAL

While Henry and the court were traveling in the north, Archbishop Cranmer had discovered shocking information about the queen. An informer had given him evidence that the queen, before her marriage, had been promiscuous first with a music teacher and later with Francis Dereham. Further investigation revealed that many knew of her indiscretions, but they had remained silent either out of fear or because they wanted to promote the relationship between Henry and Catherine. Cranmer, who supported the changes in the church, was opposed to the Howard faction, which wanted to restore Catholicism, so he agreed to take the information to the the king.

When he was faced with the scandalous news of Catherine's affairs, Henry at first thought it was just vicious gossip, and he ordered an investigation to prove that the rumors were false. When he discovered that the stories were true, Henry's emotions veered between anger and sorrow. At one moment he cried, but next he was calling for her blood. Cranmer and members of the council then went to confront the queen, who became hysterical. At first the king showed some compassion, and she was secluded but not sent to the Tower of London. When questioned, however, Dereham told his questioners that after her marriage to Henry, the queen had taken Thomas Culpepper, one of the king's closest friends, as a lover.

Henry experienced sorrow, anger, and humiliation, and he believed that Catherine had made him look like a fool. Both Culpepper and Dereham were tortured, but neither would confess to having sexual relations with Catherine after her marriage. Finally both were sentenced to the painful death of being drawn and quartered. Because of his close friendship with the king, Culpepper's sentence was later reduced to being beheaded, a more humane form of execution.

Catherine did not receive a trial but was sentenced to be beheaded. The night before she was killed, she asked that the block be brought to her rooms so that she could practice placing her head on it. On February 13, 1542, she was beheaded at the same place where her cousin, Anne Boleyn, had been executed six years earlier. To avoid future scandal, Parliament passed a law ruling that it was treasonous for a woman to marry the king if she had not led a virtuous life.

HENRY IS URGED TO REMARRY

On the day of Catherine's death, Henry celebrated by giving a supper and banquet, which was attended by many ladies of the court, and some of the courtiers watched to see if any of them might attract Henry's interest as a prospective wife. In spite of the outward gaiety, however, Catherine's deception left Henry in a state of depression. Although he had not been particularly close to his older sister Margaret, the news that she had died in Scotland also contributed to his sadness. To distract himself, he turned to overeating and added more weight to his already heavy body. During this period he read a large number of scholarly and religious books, writing his thoughts in the margins.

Within two months of Catherine's execution, Henry was being urged to consider another marriage to provide additional heirs to the throne. Anne of Cleves had moved her household to be closer to the king, and some believed that he should consider remarrying her. Although the two did exchange gifts for the New Year, their relationship was more friendly than romantic.

INTERNATIONAL TROUBLES

In November 1542 worsening relations with Scotland caused the king to send a military force under Norfolk's command to the bor-

der. The English invaded Scotland, burning farms, towns, and churches and destroying recently harvested crops. James, the Scottish king, was too sick to lead the Scots, who were easily defeated. Before the end of the year, James died. His heir was an infant girl born shortly before his death.

Henry was delighted by the birth of his great-niece, Mary, later called the Queen of Scots, and plotted for the engagement of the child with Prince Edward, a move which

Henry read many scholarly works after Catherine was executed. His handwriting is seen at the bottom of this page from a volume of Cicero.

would bring Scotland under English control. He unsuccessfully tried to obtain guardianship of the baby, but it was finally agreed that she be engaged to Edward and sent to England when she was ten. The Scots, however, did not agree to the annexation of Scotland to England.

Author N. Brysson Morrison writes:

> If Henry had been content . . . with the marriage of the Scots Queen to his son, all the patient and skilled negotiations of his former years might well have borne fruit. His deteriorating health contributed something to his diminishing statesmanship where Scotland was concerned, but he had grown into a despot and despotism and conciliation do not go hand in hand.[31]

CATHERINE PARR

Shortly after returning from the north in February 1543, Henry began to show interest in a thirty-one-year-old widow named Catherine Parr. Because she had been married to a much older man, she understood how to be a wife to the aging king. Although she was in love with another man and had no particular desire to marry Henry, who was old, fat, and often ill-tempered, she agreed to accept his offer.

Unlike Catherine Howard, Catherine Parr was not flirtatious. A serious, intelligent woman, she loved to study and to read and had strong religious viewpoints. She was also willing to be stepmother to Henry's three children. Henry and Catherine were married at Hampton Court on July 12, 1543. Both of his daughters who had recently been restored to the order of succession attended the ceremony. Shortly after the marriage Catherine wrote to her brother saying that being Henry's wife was "the greatest joy and comfort that could happen to her."[32]

Catherine proved an ideal wife for Henry. Her motto, "To be useful in all I do,"[33] describes her personality. She decorated her rooms with flowers and enjoyed her pet greyhounds and parrots, and although she was not a beauty, she dressed in French gowns. She also saw that Henry's son and daughters were well dressed. Catherine enjoyed dancing, and she was fond of music. The couple shared a common interest in religion. Catherine was particularly fond of reading religious books, and in 1545 she authored a well-received book titled *Prayers or Meditations*. Her second book, *Lamentations*, credited Henry for awakening her to a deeper religious belief. However, the book, which denounced the pope, was too controversial and was not published until after Henry's death. In addition to her own writing, she encouraged scholars to speak at court and sponsored translations of other authors' works.

Early in his sixth marriage Henry had authored another book, *A Necessary Doctrine and Erudition for Any Christian Man*, also called *The King's Book*, in which he argued for traditional practices in religion. Eustache Chapuys, ambassador to England for Emperor Charles, commented that the book proved that the Church of England only differed from Roman Catholicism in its refusal to acknowledge the power of the pope.

Henry and Catherine Parr are wed at Hampton Court in 1543. Henry's sixth and final wife proved to be one of his favorites.

Henry Again Wages War Against France

During the last years of his life, Henry waged expensive and unsuccessful wars against Scotland and France with the result of isolating England and bringing the country to bankruptcy. The first occurred near the end of 1543. Henry had hoped that negotiating an engagement between the infant Scottish princess and his son would bring Scotland under English control, but in December 1543, all treaties with England were cancelled by the Scots, who renewed

Henry VIII and Mapmaking

As a young man Henry did not believe maps to be important to efficiently running a government, but by the time of his death, maps had become an essential part of his reign. Early maps were considered to be status symbols or decorative artifacts. They were not detailed but rather were designed to present historical, biblical, and even zoological concepts. Local maps depicting regions in detail were few. After Henry's successful campaign against France in 1513, he commissioned paintings and maps to show his triumph.

It was probably Nicolaus Kratzer, the royal astronomer, who recognized the importance of maps in governance. Kratzer was from southern Germany, where accurate maps had been made since the late 1400s. John Rastel, brother-in-law of Sir Thomas More, also was an advocate for precise maps.

A new approach in English mapmaking, which emphasized realism and accuracy, was unveiled at festivities in Greenwich in 1527. A map of the world made in the new style amazed those who viewed it.

In *Henry VIII: A European Court in England,* edited by David Starkey, Peter Barber writes:

> By the time of Henry's death, maps had become accepted as the King's eyes in distant regions. Nor was there a greater cartographic enthusiast and connoisseur, nor a greater friend and recruiter of able map makers. Amidst the state papers in his private library in Whitehall, there were drawers full of "plats" and plentiful instruments for their creation as well as utilization. Droughtsmen [draftsmen] regularly came to Greenwich to make neat vellum copies of Henry's own sketch maps and engineers were called from France to explain their plats in person. His privy gallery was filled with grander maps displaying his and his allies' kingdoms, his territorial omniscience, his victories and his claims.
>
> In barely twenty years and in large part in response to his wishes, maps had become an indispensible tool of English government.

their alliances with France. Henry was furious and ordered an invasion of Scotland to capture the princess and bring her to England. Although the army caused much destruction in Scotland, they were unable to find the princess, whom the Scots had carefully hidden. Henry had to delay further fighting with Scotland because he now planned to invade France.

By the beginning of 1544 the relations between France and England had worsened, and Henry prepared to lead the invasion in spite of his ill health. The ulcer in his leg had caused him to suffer fever and pain, and he often was seen resting his sore leg in Catherine's lap. His advisers and doctors were very worried about his ability to make such a strenuous trip, but Henry, who had always enjoyed the excitement of battle, insisted—even though he had to be lifted onto his horse and wear armor that was cut away from his swollen leg.

Before he left, Parliament passed a new Act of Succession in case Henry, now fifty-three years old, did not survive the campaign. The new rule made Edward and any children he might have first in the line of succession. They were followed by Princess Mary and her heirs, and thirdly by Princess Elizabeth. In Henry's absence, Catherine had been named regent of England.

Henry and the English troops landed in France in July for what would be his last campaign. Henry's desire was to capture the city of Boulogne, which in September fell to the English. Henry then returned to England, but the hostilities continued.

The following spring the French threatened an invasion of England in a move to force Henry to return Boulogne. The king's council urged Henry to give the French what they wanted, but he stubbornly refused. Finally a treaty was agreed upon on June 7, 1546, in which Henry was allowed to keep Boulogne for eight more years after which time it would return to France. The expensive wars had not resolved the struggles with Scotland, and England's position in regard to France and the Holy Roman Empire was still unsettled.

RELIGIOUS CONFUSION AND DISSENSION

While England struggled with problems with France and Scotland, the country was also torn by disputes between the competing religious factions. Henry expected that his people would support the new ideas of the Church of England without question, but many challenged them. Author Carolly Erickson writes: "The clerics who refused to instruct believers in the new doctrines, the individuals who refused to learn the Lord's Prayer and Creed in English, clinging to the Latin they had learned in youth, the staunch Protestants who rejected the royal injunctions because they stopped short of a thoroughgoing break with the past—all these people defied the king."[34]

The king and Catherine often discussed religion, but sometimes her viewpoint, which seemed sympathetic to Protestantism, irritated Henry, who opposed ideas that he considered to be radical. During the first half of 1546, two of his advisers had directed witch hunts against the Protestants, and they took advantage of Henry's irritation to attack the queen, saying that they could prove she was a dangerous heretic. Henry agreed to sign papers accusing her of treasonous heresy.

When word of this accusation reached Catherine, she hurried to see Henry and beg his forgiveness, promising that she would be obedient to him in everything. She said that she had only discussed different religious ideas to distract him from the pain in his leg. Henry answered, "Is it even so, sweetheart? . . . Then perfect friends we are now again as ever at any time heretofore."[35] The next day, when the king and queen were together in their gardens, the lord chancellor and a group of guards came to arrest her, but Henry drove them off angrily.

Although Catherine managed to escape the witch hunt, several others were arrested and burned at the stake for their ideas.

THE FINAL DAYS OF THE KING

During 1546 Henry suffered greatly from his painful leg, and he could no longer go up and down stairs. In spite of his suffering, his mind was active, and he continued reading and he ordered new books, calendars, and almanacs. It is believed that Catherine had convinced him to wear glasses for reading, and he ordered ten pairs at a time. When he could, he enjoyed walking in his gardens, where he had instructed four thousand rosebushes planted, and he cared for his menagerie of pets, including canaries, ferrets, beagles, hounds, and spaniels.

In December 1546 Henry suffered from a serious fever, and he decided to spend the holidays in London. Not wanting his family to be at his bedside, he ordered the queen and the court to Greenwich. Rumors about the king's poor health spread.

Because it was treason to predict the death of the king, no one dared to discuss the subject with Henry. Finally on January 27, 1547, Sir Anthony Denny, one of the gentlemen of his chamber, told him that he was seriously ill and probably would not live long. Henry asked that Archbishop Cranmer come to see him, but he said he first wanted to sleep for awhile. When Cranmer finally arrived, Henry could no longer speak, but he squeezed the archbishop's hand when asked if he trusted in Christ. A short time later, at about two in the morning on Friday, January 28, 1547, Henry VIII died.

Following his death, his body was embalmed and was laid in state until February 14, when it was taken to Windsor to be buried at St. George's Chapel next to Jane Seymour, the wife he honored as mother to his heir.

THE IMPORTANCE OF HENRY VIII

Henry had been a legend in his own time and remains one of the most famous of all English monarchs. He did many cruel things during his reign, but he also made many lasting contributions. Although it caused much dissension and resulted in many executions, one of his most significant accomplishments was establishing the Church of England, a move that ultimately

THE GRAVES OF HENRY AND HIS WIVES

The final resting places of the immediate family of Henry VIII are in various sites around England. King Henry and Jane Seymour are interred together in St. George's Chapel, Windsor. The two wives who were beheaded, Anne Boleyn and Catherine Howard, are buried close together. After their executions, their decapitated bodies were taken to the Chapel of St. Peter ad Vincula in the Tower of London and buried in unmarked graves. In 1876 the chapel was restored. With the approval of Queen Victoria, the remains of the two queens were exhumed and reburied under the marble pavement in front of the altar. Plaques now tell their names and the dates of their deaths.

Anne of Cleves is buried in Westminster Abbey to the south of the high altar near where British monarchs are crowned. Letters mark the spot saying, "Anne of Cleves. Queen of England. Born 1515. Died 1557." Catherine Parr is buried at Sudeley. After years of neglect, her grave is marked by a marble effigy.

The most honored grave is that of Catherine of Aragon, Henry's first wife. At her death she had been reduced to the title of Princess Dowager, a title she rejected. She is buried at the Cathedral of Peterborough. Neglected for years, her grave was restored in 1891, when a memorial was installed. It was inscribed with her coat of arms, a pomegranate and a cross. The plaque reads, "Katherine Queen of England." In 1986, the 450th anniversary of her burial, the Spanish government presented a new royal standard bearing the queen's emblems. A tablet reads, "A queen cherished by the English People for her Loyalty, Piety, Courage and Compassion." The tomb is regularly marked by flowers placed there by anonymous visitors who honor her memory and respect the integrity she showed as queen of England.

ended England's religious dependence on Rome.

Many historians agree that Henry VIII brought England out of the Middle Ages and laid the foundation for a modern state. His use of Parliament to accomplish his objectives increased the power of that legislative body in England and ultimately led to the parliamentary form of government that exists there today. When he was born, the country was just emerging from many bloody years of civil unrest as various factions vied for control of the monarchy. Although he was not successful in bringing Scotland under English control, Henry was able to put much of the political intrigue in his own country down by executing those who challenged his authority to rule. He enhanced the prestige and power of the monarchy and made England a country that other European powers of the time took seriously.

Henry also made a significant contribution to the arts. Although much of what he

King Henry VIII made many lasting contributions to English society, and he remains one of history's most famous monarchs.

tures, manuscripts, jewelry, scientific instruments, books, and maps made under his orders. Also remaining are examples of his poetry and musical compositions.

On the negative side, many people were unjustly executed during his reign. He also confiscated much of the money from monasteries and convents, but instead of using it to help his people, he squandered it on unsuccessful wars. The fortune he inherited from his father disappeared, and at his death, Henry was in debt.

Henry spent much of his reign worrying about the succession to the throne after his death. All three of his children eventually reigned over England. After his death, his ten-year-old son became King Edward VI. Never a healthy child, he died of tuberculosis in 1553 just before his sixteenth birthday. Henry's two daughters became the first women to rule England as queen. His older daughter, Mary, succeeded her brother as queen. Her determination to restore Catholicism in England resulted in so much violence that she is known as Bloody Mary. Henry's daughter Elizabeth, the last of the Tudors, is considered to be one of England's finest monarchs, transforming the country into one of Europe's greatest powers.

built and sponsored has been lost—of his fifty-five palaces, only Hampton Court and St. James still exist—many works of art and architecture remain. There are many significant examples of stained glass, minia-

Notes

Introduction: A King Without Equals

1. Quoted in Antonia Fraser, *The Wives of Henry VIII.* New York: Vintage Books, 1994, p. 1.

2. E.W. Ives, *Anne Boleyn.* Oxford: Basil Blackwell, 1986, pp. 55–56.

Chapter 1: A Royal Childhood, 1491–1509

3. Carolly Erickson, *Great Harry.* New York: St. Martin's Griffin, 1980, pp. 25–26.

4. Quoted in Roberta Strauss Feuerlicht, *The Life and World of Henry VIII.* New York: Crowell-Collier Press, 1970, p. 7.

5. N. Brysson Morrison, *The Private Life of Henry VIII.* New York: Vanguard Press, 1964, p. 28.

Chapter 2: The Young King Brings Promise of New Prosperity, 1509–1513

6. Quoted in Alison Weir, *Henry VIII: The King and His Court.* New York: Ballantine Books, 2001, p. 21.

7. Quoted in Erickson, *Great Harry,* p. 56.

8. Derek Wilson, *In the Lion's Court.* New York: St. Martin's Press, 2001, p. 71.

9. Erickson, *Great Harry,* p. 60.

10. Erickson, *Great Harry,* p. 75.

Chapter 3: Political Intrigues and a Lust for Power, 1514–1523

11. Quoted in Erickson, *Great Harry,* p. 91.

12. Morrison, *The Private Life of Henry VIII,* p. 48.

13. Quoted in Morrison, *The Private Life of Henry VIII,* p. 51.

14. Erickson, *Great Harry,* p. 134.

15. Quoted in Weir, *Henry VIII,* p. 223.

Chapter 4: The Death of a Cardinal and the King's "Great Matter," 1520–1530

16. Quoted in Maria Perry, *The Sisters of Henry VIII.* New York: St. Martin's Press, 1998, p. 175.

17. Erickson, *Great Harry,* p. 158.

18. Quoted in Morrison, *The Private Life of Henry VIII,* p. 79.

19. Quoted in Fraser, *The Wives of Henry VIII,* p. 130.

20. Fraser, *The Wives of Henry VIII,* p. 138.

21. Quoted in Erickson, *Great Harry,* p. 228.

Chapter 5: Henry Defines the Church, 1530–1535

22. Morrison, *The Private Life of Henry VIII,* pp. 99–100.

23. Weir, *Henry VIII,* p. 293.

24. Quoted in *The Six Wives of Henry VIII,* video. Granada Bristol Productions, Thirteen/WNET Television, New York: Educational Broadcasting Corporation, 2003.

25. Erickson, *Great Harry,* p. 243.

26. Quoted in Erickson, *Great Harry,* p. 253.

Chapter 6: To Arouse the King's Anger Means Death, 1535–1540

27. Morrison, *The Private Life of Henry VIII,* p. 128.

28. Weir, *Henry VIII,* pp. 368–69.

29. Fraser, *The Wives of Henry VIII*, p. 228.

Chapter 7: The Final Years, 1540–1547

30. Fraser, *The Wives of Henry VIII*, p. 333.

31. Morrison, *The Private Life of Henry VIII*, p. 187.

32. Quoted in Erickson, *Great Harry*, p. 333.

33. Quoted in Fraser, *The Wives of Henry VII*, p. 371.

34. Erickson, *Great Harry*, p. 356.

35. Quoted in Feuerlicht, *The Life and World of Henry VIII*, p. 145.

For Further Reading

Books

Frank Dwyer, *Henry VIII*. New York: Chelsea House, 1998. This is a young adult biography about the life and times of Henry VIII.

Philippa Gregory, *The Other Boleyn Girl*. New York: Scribner Paperbacks, 2002. This novel relates incidents in the life of Anne Boleyn's older sister, Mary, who was a mistress of Henry VIII.

Mary Luke, *The Ivy Crown*. New York: Doubleday, 1984. This novel tells the story of Henry's last wife, Catherine Parr.

Rosemary Menard, *Long Meg*. New York: Pantheon, 1982. Meg, a tall innkeeper's daughter, dons her father's clothes and joins the army of Henry VIII for the invasion of France. The book is for young readers.

Carolyn Meyer, *Doomed Queen Anne*. San Diego: Gulliver Books, 2002. A novelized telling of the love affair between Anne Boleyn and Henry VIII, this book is written for teens. Other books about the young Tudors in the Young Royals series are *Beware, Princess Elizabeth*, and *Mary, Bloody Mary*.

Jean Plaidy, *Murder Most Royal*. New York: Putnam, 1972. This novel focuses on the executions of Anne Boleyn and Catherine Howard.

Judith Merkle Riley, *The Serpent Garden*. New York: Viking, 1996. The protagonist, a young widow, is commissioned as an artist by Thomas Wolsey and goes to Paris for the marriage of Henry's sister Mary to the king of France. The readable book, written by a professor at Claremont McKenna College, contains many details about life in the early sixteenth century.

Plays

Maxwell Anderson, *Anne of the Thousand Days*. New York: Dramatists Play Service, 1977. Set against the court of Henry VIII, the play depicts the relationship of Henry VIII and Anne Boleyn.

Robert Bolt, *A Man for All Seasons*, in *Plays of Our Time*, ed. Bennett Cerf. New York: Random House, 1967. An insightful play about the life and death of Sir Thomas More.

William Shakespeare, *Henry VIII*, in *The Works of William Shakespeare*. Cambridge, England: Cambridge University Press, 1962. A classic play about Henry VIII's struggles to divorce Catherine and marry Anne Boleyn.

J.C. Trewin, ed., *Six Wives of Henry VIII*. New York: Frederick Ungar, 1972. Six plays produced by the British Broadcasting Corporation in 1970.

Films and Videos

Anne of 1000 Days, video. MCA Home Video, 1994. A film version of the Maxwell Anderson play, this movie was nominated for many Academy Awards. It depicts the reign and death of Anne Boleyn.

The Six Wives of Henry VIII, video. Granada Bristol Productions, Thirteen/WNET Television, New York: Educational Broadcasting Corporation, 2003.

Web Sites

Luminarium (www.luminarium.org). This Web site contains biographies and sketches of many people and events important in the life of Henry VIII, including Sir Thomas More, Desiderius Erasmus, and Thomas Wolsey. It also plays music from the sixteenth century.

Englishhistory.net (http://englishhistory. net). This Web site includes excerpts from the love letters written by Henry VIII to Anne Boleyn.

University of Toronto Libraries (http://eir. library.utoronto.ca). A Web site that includes representative poetry written by Henry VIII.

Historical Royal Palaces (www.hrp.org.uk). A Web site of historical royal places, including Hampton Court and the Tower of London.

Works Consulted

Books

Robert Bolt, *A Man for All Seasons*, in *Plays of Our Time*, ed. Bennett Cerf. New York: Random House, 1967. This prize-winning Broadway play, first produced in 1961, tells of the challenges of conscience and downfall of Sir Thomas More.

Carolly Erickson, *Great Harry*. New York: St. Martin's Griffin, 1980. This is a detailed and comprehensive biography of Henry VIII's life and times.

Roberta Strauss Feuerlicht, *The Life and World of Henry VIII*. New York: Crowell-Collier Press, 1970. A readable biography of Henry VIII, this book contains interesting quotes from his associates.

Antonia Fraser, *The Wives of Henry VIII*. New York: Vintage Books, 1994. Lady Antonia Fraser reveals the human dimensions of the six wives of Henry VIII, along with an insight into the period.

Antonia Fraser, ed., *The Lives of the Kings and Queens of England*. Berkeley: University of California Press, 1975. This volume recounts the lives of every English ruler from 1066 to the end of the twentieth century.

Michael Glenne, *Henry VIII's Fifth Wife: The Story of Catherine Howard*. New York: Robert M. McBride, 1948. A detailed, though somewhat romanticized biography of Henry's youngest wife.

E.W. Ives, *Anne Boleyn*. Oxford: Basil Blackwell, 1986. This biography of Henry's second wife tells of her early life and education, her often turbulent association with Henry, and her downfall.

N. Brysson Morrison, *The Private Life of Henry VIII*. New York: Vanguard Press, 1964. The author reveals Henry's private life with intimacy and ease.

Maria Perry, *The Sisters of Henry VIII*. New York: St. Martin's Press, 1998. The book discusses the tumultuous lives of Henry's sisters, Margaret of Scotland and Mary of France.

Lacey Baldwin Smith, *Henry VIII: The Mask of Royalty*. Chicago: Academy Chicago, 1987. A well-documented study of the character and personality of Henry VIII.

David Starkey, *Six Wives: The Queens of Henry VIII*. New York: HarperCollins, 2003. A detailed study of Henry VIII's wives, the book examines the rituals of marriage, diplomacy, pregnancy, and religion in the Tudor Court.

David Starkey, ed., *Henry VIII: A European Court in England*. New York: Cross River Press, 1991. This anthology of the arts, history, and culture of Henry VIII's court is lavishly illustrated with color photographs and drawings.

Alison Weir, *Henry VIII: The King and His Court.* New York: Ballantine Books, 2001. A readable biography of Henry VIII, with many interesting details about his life.

Derek Wilson, *In the Lion's Court.* New York: St. Martin's Press, 2001. The author tells of the lives of six prominent men in Henry's court whose ambitions led to death and executions.

Periodical

Ralph Turner, "The Meaning of the Magna Carta Since 1215," *History Today,* September 2003.

Index

Act in Restraint of
　Appeals, 68, 71
Act of Supremacy, 71
Acts of Succession, 72, 95
Adagia (Erasmus), 17
Adrian VI (pope), 51
Amicable Grant, 52
Anglicanism, 71
Anne Boleyn (Ives), 12
Anne of Cleves, 84, 91, 97
Arthur Tudor (brother)
　appearance of, 16
　death of, 20
　marriage of, 19–20, 25,
　　60
　relationship of, to
　　Henry VIII, 13
arts, 85, 94, 97–98
　see also music
Aske, Robert, 82
Assertio (Henry VIII), 50
astronomy, 18, 76

Barber, Peter, 94
Beaufort, Lady Margaret
　(grandmother), 19, 27
Black Book, 51
Blount, Elizabeth, 41, 43,
　46
Boleyn, Anne (Nan), 54
　characteristics of, 66, 70
　crowned, 68–70
　downfall of, 77–79
　grave of, 97
　love for, 55, 58, 62,
　　65–68

marriage of, 67, 76
as mistress, 67
pregnancies of, 75, 76
religious beliefs of,
　66–67, 71
unpopularity of, 69–70,
　75
Boleyn, George, 77–78, 79
Boleyn, Mary, 48
Bolt, Robert, 65
Bosworth Field, battle of,
　13, 14
Brandon, Charles
　boyhood of, 19
　Mary Tudor and, 38
　power of, 37
　war against France and,
　　52
Buckingham, Duke of, 49

Calais (France), 14, 22
Campeggio, Cardinal, 59
Catherine of Aragon
　appearance of, 19, 41
　Blount and, 43
　Church of England and,
　　72–73
　crowned, 26–27
　death of, 75–76
　Fitzroy and, 55
　grave of, 97
　health of, 42, 62
　influence of
　　loss of, 38, 56, 67
　　as regent, 33–34,
　　　35–36

marriage of, to Arthur,
　19–20, 25, 60
marriage of, to Henry,
　10, 25, 76
　annulment of, 53,
　　56–57, 58–59, 60–61,
　　67
　negotiations for,
　　20–21, 23–24
popularity of, 48, 60, 62
pregnancies of, 30–31,
　34, 40, 41, 42
Catholic Church
　Charles V and, 39, 57,
　　58, 59, 83
　in England
　　attacks on, 72–74, 81,
　　　83
　　Cranmer and, 90
　　Cromwell and, 70–71
　　influence of, 32
　　More and, 64
　　power of Henry VIII
　　　and, 11–12, 64–65,
　　　68, 71
　　support for, 81–83, 87,
　　　95–96
　in France, 39
　Francis I and, 83
　Henry VIII as defender
　　of, 49–50, 65
　importance of, 11
　marriages and, 20, 56, 57
　see also Reformation
Chapuys, Eustache,
　66–67, 80, 92

Picture Credits

About the Author

Marilyn Tower Oliver is the author of more than 250 articles for adults and children, which have appeared in national and regional publications such as the *Los Angeles Times, Dolls,* and *Valley Magazine,* where she is a contributing editor. She has also written seven books for young adults including *Natural Crafts* and *The Importance of Muhammad* (Lucent Books, 2003). She also produces and hosts a southern California cable television talk show about opera called *Opera! Opera! Opera!* Oliver is a distinguished graduate of Stanford University where she also received a master of arts degree in secondary education. She lives in Los Angeles with two poodles and a Siamese cat.